Becoming the Most Valuable Professional in Your Tech Community

PABLO PERALTA

Xelentia Ltd.

Atlantida, Canelones, Uruguay

First published 2020
by Xelentia Ltd.
Atlantida, Canelones, Uruguay
www.becomemvp.com
© 2020 by Pablo Peralta

Library of Congress Cataloging-in-Publication Data

ISBN paperback: 978-1-7351925-1-2
ISBN hardback: 978-1-7351925-2-9
ISBN ebook: 978-1-7351925-0-5

"MVP means a passion for innovation, supporting the community, and networking with the greatest international talent. All of this changed my professional career forever, thanks to the mentorship of Pablo Peralta."

Pablo J. Moreno, Microsoft MVP
DELL EMC Data Scientific

"We're here to put a dent in the universe. Otherwise why else even be here?"

Steve Jobs

To you, for making tech communities an extraordinary place to connect, learn, and share.

To my family and every family supporting MVPs and aspirants in their efforts to make a difference in this world.

Contents

ABOUT THIS BOOK

"This is the book I should have written. Being an MVP previously and now managing an MVP Program, I can tell that this is the best summary so far how becoming an MVP works. The attitude and passion are key attributes for anyone who Is considering to step on this road. Debunking the myths and avoiding the pitfalls can help to move on faster, while having a strategy is essential to get there. Sharing your knowledge and experience is the most rewarding thing on Earth, so even if you do not want to be an MVP, read this book to become a more valuable community member."

Tamas Varga

Manager of the MVP Program at Sitecore

Sitecore MVP 2010–2016

Becoming the Most Valuable Professional in Your Tech Community provides you with the principles and strategies to apply, the most common mistakes to avoid, habits to develop, and secrets you need to know to truly transcend boundaries in your career and become a better you by positively impacting others.

This book includes these essentials for your success:

- Core principles and values to incorporate for your MVP journey

- Ways to communicate the benefits of being an MVP to employers

- Myths about MVPs, what it takes, and who can be one

- Common pitfalls MVP aspirants need to avoid

- The four strategic pillars that will help you reach your MVP goals

- Key steps to take in your journey toward your nomination (and renewal)

- How nomination processes work according to most vendors and what you need to consider before getting nominated

- Advice on how to make the most of your MVP powers

Whether you aspire to become a thought leader, get recognized and keep relevant in the Microsoft community, Salesforce, Sitecore, Embarcadero, SAP, Oracle, Google, AWS, or any other, it doesn't matter. I wrote this book so it takes you beyond any vendor's recognition or award.

As a bonus, **Take Action!** sections have been included in this book to help you put what you learn into practice and tailor your MVP strategy and journey.

Why I wrote this book

Communities made me who I am today, and I feel blessed every day for being able to dedicate part of my life to them.

I've been involved in tech communities since I was just a teenager in the '90s learning how to code and sharing my ideas with others when the Internet was far from what we know today. Since then, I've never stopped joining and developing new communities to openly share knowledge, get mutual help, and forge long-lasting friendships.

I remember with sympathy incurring in some antics to avoid being discovered by my bosses spending so much time in communities, usually helping others in forums, because that made me happy and let me learn more every day. I used to install those programs that let you quickly switch between one window and another with simple keyword shortcuts among other techniques to avoid being discovered. Of course, I didn't always succeed, and some days I returned home a bit scolded.

Nevertheless, I insisted on participating in communities every day and learning more about the technologies I loved—e.g., I'm among those who tried first betas of Microsoft. Net platform in the early 2000s. I committed to attending every local event, even when it cost me some big money for my little pockets and asking for permission from my bosses. Without a doubt, they were my best investments; I not only learned a lot, but I also met extraordinary people with whom I cultivated true long-lasting friendship (and made some businesses later as well). I also met my first employer in the Microsoft ecosystem, which used to sponsor some of those events.

So, at that time, my life started to transform, thanks to participating in communities. In my early twenties, and with no university degree at all, I found myself blessed by working in fascinating software projects with some of those gurus I used to see speaking at events, traveling to other countries and meeting amazing new people. And it all started by getting involved in communities.

Thanks to my employer for sponsoring and sometimes even organizing events; it encouraged their employees to go out and speak, to share knowledge in the community. That's how I started speaking at events. In the beginning, it was weird, and I felt uncomfortable—truly out of my comfort zone—but it was so gratifying to share with others my passion, what I was learning about the technologies I was using. I am thankful that gratitude prevailed over my fears about speaking.

Again, the power of the community was just marvelous. It was transforming me into a more fulfilled person.

As years passed, I moved to other jobs. I founded some companies, created some software products, and always kept myself participating in communities, both offline and online—fortunately with an Internet a little bit closer as we know it today.

In 2008, I was curios and decided to specialize in one software technology for business that was emerging fast—Microsoft Dynamics. After learning a little bit and getting certified, I realized at that time that there was very little information (especially in Spanish—my native language), leaving some people like me with questions unanswered.

So, guess what? I had the epiphany that what was missing was a community, so I decided to create one during nights and weekends. Yes, and that was the beginning of Comunidad365—later acquired by Dynamic Communities, Inc.—a community to connect, exchange ideas, and learn about Microsoft Dynamics, encompassing thousands of Spanish-speaking people from all places. It started from scratch and ended up exchanging thousands of forum posts, sharing hundreds of webinars, tens of compelling pieces of training, and local events.

Without expecting anything in return and with very little idea about the Most Valuable Professional (MVP) program, I was first officially recognized by Microsoft as an MVP in 2010 for my contributions. Having enjoyed the same grace over the last 9 consecutive years, I can promise you that if you love technology, hanging out with like-minded people, and positively impacting your community, the MVP journey is priceless.

I just can't express how blessed I feel and how getting involved in communities transformed me into who I am today, having so many fantastic friends in the world who are extraordinary persons and talented professionals.

Some of them sought my advice on how to become an MVP, and luckily, I found myself being useful, helping them to explore their talents, put them at the service of their communities, and in the end, those who persevered became nominated and part of the MVP family as well. I cherish the celebration of those awards much more than I do mine.

However, I realized that I started becoming repetitive in my advice and that the one-on-one mentoring model didn't scale. Indeed, I started to feel selfish by not sharing what I had learned over the years in a broader way. Not to mention all those who encouraged me to write a book on the subject!

After some research, as at the time of this writing, I couldn't find any other similar book or compelling craft about how and what it truly means to become an MVP. So, seduced by the challenge, I embraced this mission and ended up with this book. In it, I aim to inspire and help you succeed in your desire to become a better you, one who is recognized as an authority, by positively impacting your tech community and by believing in golden principles like sharing knowledge, helping others to succeed, and providing solutions without expecting anything in return.

I hope you find this book useful. Enjoy your MVP journey and live an extraordinary MVP life!

Why you should read this book

The privileges you will enjoy, the amazing people you will meet, the new resources you will unlock, the extraordinary opportunities that will knock on your door, the new projects you had always imagined working on, and best of all, the positive impact you will generate in others' careers will both professionally and personally let you vibrate in a whole new frequency.

And that's only part of what happens when you become a Most Valuable Professional (MVP) or whatever your technology vendor calls it (e.g., ACE, Champion, Expert, Hero).

Becoming an MVP is transformative. It's not a destination in itself but an amazing avenue for you to become a better person and professional.

Whether you are an MVP aspirant, a current MVP, a former MVP, or not sure but curious about what it is, this book will help light your fire and find the guidance you need to achieve and maintain your MVP status.

While my experience has always been as a Microsoft MVP, I have designed the principles, strategies, and every lesson in this book so that it broadly applies to any technology vendor.

In reality, this book goes beyond any technology vendor and community awards program. Indeed, it will touch the way you live your professional career and how you want to take it to the top in the best gratifying manner: making a difference in your community.

Sitecore MVPs enjoying the NBA Experience during the 2019 MVP Summit in Orlando, Florida—courtesy of Tamas Varga, Manager of the MVP Program at Sitecore.

DOWNLOAD YOUR MVP LOG & PLANNER
SPREADSHEET FREE OF CHARGE NOW!

Being a great contributor in your community, while necessary, is not enough for those aspiring to become an MVP or get renewed. You also need to prove it.

That is why keeping records of ALL your contributions and their positive impact is as critical as the act of contributing.

I've created a simple but effective spreadsheet for you to use to log and plan your community activities so you can have a concrete picture of your current progress, set up your future goals, and have in one place the information you need when you get nominated for the MVP award—or whatever name your vendor calls it.

You can download it free of charge from here:

www.becomemvp.com

	A	B	C	D	E	F	G	
1	**My MVP Log & Planner**							
2	Completed and In-Progress Contributions							
3	Title	Primary Technology / Product	Status	Publish date	Contribution Type	Link to Activity	Impact: # Views / # Attendees / # Downloads	Comment
4	Blog post / magazine article / book title	< Generally, this entry will always be the same.>		2019-11-27	Writing	https://my-blog/my-article	120	
5	Conference / user group meeting / other community event			2019-10-08	Speaking	https://my-conference	200	
6	Your local user group / community development activity			2019-09-09	Leadership	https://my-user-group-meeting	400	
7	Webinar or video production title			2019-08-29		youtube/my-video	820	
8	Open source project name			2019-07-24	Community Project	https://github/my-project	550	
9	Forum name			2019-06-10	Forum Contribution	https://my-forum-profile	340	
10	Other			2019-05-27	Other	https://any-forum-profile	630	
11							3060	
12	Planned Contributions							
13	Name		Status	Planned date	Contribution Type	Link to Activity	Planned Impact	Comment
14	User group meeting planned for				Leadership			
15	Record a course about ...		Waiting for Instructions					
16	Speak at a conference.		Planned		Speaking			
17								
18	Upcoming & Ideas Pool							
19	Name		Status	Planned date	Contribution Type	Link to activity	Planned Impact	Comment
20	Launch a community / special interest group in my local language.							
21	Record a course about							

Become MVP   +

From that same site, you will also find additional training and resources to support your MVP journey as I make them available.

Make sure to subscribe so you're first to know when I release something new.

1 INTRODUCTION

"Give the world the best you have, and the best will come back to you."

Madeline Bridges

Becoming a recognized and awarded professional by a tech vendor is not a career path for everyone but may be right for you if you are passionate enough and ready to take your career to higher levels.

In this introductory chapter, you'll learn what makes these professionals extraordinary, their distinguishing characteristics and behaviors according to relevant tech vendors like Microsoft, Salesforce, Sitecore, Embarcadero, SAP, Oracle, Google, and Amazon.

Besides, you'll get an overview of what it takes to become awarded according to most of the vendors, the benefits you will enjoy, how to convince your employer to support you, and how nomination processes commonly work.

Who are MVPs?

Most Valuable Professionals, or MVPs, are technology experts who passionately share their knowledge with the community. That's the simplest but most powerful definition as extracted from the Microsoft MVP program's website.

Salesforce MVP program highlights characteristics of these extraordinary individuals such us Expertise, Generosity, Leadership, and Advocacy.

Sitecore reinforces the community spirit of their MVPs, defining them as individuals with expertise in Sitecore who actively participate in online and offline communities to share their knowledge and expertise with other Sitecore partners and customers.

Embarcadero refers to their MVPs as the "best of the best" of their community members and trusted assets for their customers and prospects.

SAP calls them *Champions* who are among the top contributors within the SAP Community and leaders who distinguish themselves in the eyes of their peers, upholding the ideals and spirit of the community.

Oracle refers to them as *ACEs*, Google as *Developer Experts*, Amazon (AWS) as *Heroes*.

The program's name could vary from vendor to vendor and over time, but the essence doesn't. *Most Valuable Professionals, or MVPs, Champions, ACEs, Experts, Heroes* **are all extraordinary professionals driven by passion about their vendor's products and sharing knowledge with their communities. Their expertise**

in their vendor's products combined with their support and contributions to their communities makes them recognized as thought leaders in their field wherever they go.

With the best aim of making it easier for you, the reader of this book, and given it's usually the most common adopted denomination worldwide, not only in the tech industry but also in sports where the original name comes from, I will simply use *MVPs* most of the time in this book. But the concepts I'm sharing will be useful, whether you are thinking of becoming an *MVP*, a *Champion*, an *ACE*, an *Expert*, a *Hero*, or whatever name your vendor uses.

In the event you're already a recognized individual by your vendor, through this book, you will reinforce several key concepts and extract several useful ideas as well to keep your fire up and maintain your status.

What does it take to become an MVP?

MVPs are independent experts, which means they're not companies but individuals going beyond their daily duties to contribute to their community, both offline and online. Usually, MVPs cannot be employees of the vendor, only external to it. They're proven, recognized influential experts making up a cohort of elite professionals worldwide.

MVPs are known for both knowledge and helping others. They are commonly considered as a trusted source for unbiased expert-level information about a technology or software product. They are the best evangelizers.

Good MVPs are close to people, love volunteering and providing help just for the sake of it. That's why they're remarkable and get officially awarded by their tech vendor.

You see them as key influencers speaking at conferences, instructing workshops, delivering webinars, organizing meet-ups, participating on expert panels, leading user groups, writing valuable articles, answering questions in forums, leading open-source initiatives and in many others spaces where they can share their passion and knowledge with others.

Due to their passion, their great contributions, and positive impact in the community, MVPs are typically a source of inspiration for others and elevate everyone around them. They are natural leaders and innate champions.

In essence, dissecting what it takes to become an MVP according to different vendors, we can identify 5 common key elements:

- Committing to learning more every day about your vendor's products

- Loving what you do and helping others

- Contributing and sharing knowledge with the community

- Leading and being a positive influencer

- And finally, as an inevitable consequence of persistently doing all of the above, getting nominated by someone else.

These elements summarize the philosophy as well as the common behaviors that make MVPs, and you will learn more about them in the upcoming chapters.

Becoming an MVP is not a career path for everyone but may be right for you. Indeed, if you love your technology and are truly passionate about sharing knowledge and creating a positive impact within your community, becoming an MVP is something you should explore and venture into. **It's fulfilling, exhilarating, and will significantly benefit you, your company, your community, and your technology vendor.**

What are the benefits?

Aside from the public recognition for their great contributions, MVPs usually enjoy exclusive benefits from their vendors such as:

- Early access to new versions of their favorite products

- Privileged training opportunities and early access to new certification programs

- Exclusive invitations to their annual MVP Summit conference and other offline and online MVP-only exciting events

- Access to classified information from their vendors

- Preferred help and support, enjoying a direct communication channel with their vendor's product teams

- Access to cool internal demos and resources

- Support and resources for running their community events

- Opportunities to speak at their vendor's conferences and events

- Discounts from their vendor to attend their conferences, buying stuff in their stores, and so on

- Lots of cool free stuff, from software subscriptions to online publications, not only from their vendor but sometimes from other third-parties too

Besides, because they are so trusted and influential, they usually receive very interesting project opportunities and are paid better than average professionals working in similar positions.

The benefits will depend on your vendor's program and may vary over time. The above list is just a compilation of some common benefits based on most vendors' programs at the time of this writing. Make sure to stay updated through your vendor's website and/or ask your Community Program Manager.

There are countless indirect benefits too. You will learn more about how to leverage your MVP powers after you get awarded later in this book in *Chapter 6 – Your MVP Powers*.

How to convince your employer

The MVP award is given by technology vendors to individuals—actual professionals, not companies. So, if you're an employee, why would your manager or company encourage you to go for it?

You may be required to spend some business hours doing community stuff and may need to request an additional budget for traveling and making it to events. Besides, you gain more exposure, with the associated risk of having competitors offer you a better salary and position. You may ask for more money after you get the award, and you may create even deeper connections with your vendor and customers than your manager has—and the list goes on. So, why would your employer support you?

Well, there are several reasons why your employer should and will support you on your journey to becoming an MVP. Reasons range from an honest desire to contribute to your professional growth to knowing that if you don't get support, you'll pursue it anyway because you feel the fire inside you.

Employers also may know that if they don't support you, you may leave them shortly and find another employer that will understand the value of having an MVP within his or her team.

If you want to become an MVP, that means you want to get better in what you do, and you're passionate about your product or technology. That's the best thing that could happen to any employer because you're pushing yourself and others around you toward improvement and success.

From a business perspective, your employer will support you because, through you becoming an MVP, you will bring more business and more money to the company. Period.

Having an MVP within the team means a competitive advantage that can be mentioned in every sales pitch, every proposal, and every marketing campaign. It's like saying to customers, "I've got a best-in-class, world-recognized professional" or "We've got a direct line to the vendor's product team."

You, as an MVP, will also operate like your vendor's insider, fully aware of what's going on with your product and what's coming up in the next version, and you will be able to try bits of the product before anybody else. So, that's a huge competitive advantage that can win customers, save your employer tons of money, as well as help your team to make better decisions within projects.

Being an MVP also means you'll be a source of leads. You will be constantly evangelizing about your product in several stages, from conferences to blogs, forums, and social networks. If your participation is associated with your company's brand, it means you're the company's best marketing weapon ever. Companies struggle and spend a lot of money trying to create valuable content to gain credibility and attract more leads these days, and that's something you will be doing for them at minimum or no direct cost at all.

What's more, as you become better known because of your contributions and great content, you'll be like a magnet that will attract not only potential customers but also amazing talent that will want to work with you as well as your company. That means a lot of money and time saved in recruiting the right people to join your company.

So, there are many reasons why you should be supported by your employer on this journey.

"Ask and it will be given to you; seek and you will find; knock and the door will be opened to you."

Matthew 7:7

Use your best judgment to determine when to knock your boss' or upper management's door, and don't be afraid of asking for support. Assuming they're smart, and your message is properly delivered, you should easily get the support you need. Believe me that the universe will be backing you up if becoming an MVP is in the path of your mission in this world.

However, in the event you don't get the support you desire, I advise you don't get stuck. Nobody can stop you if you have the burning desire to excel in your professional career and your life. It's yours in the end.

I had some hard times in my past getting support when I was employed by someone else. It was never easy, but I persisted and did most of my MVP learning at my own expense, and it was absolutely worthwhile.

In the event you're self-employed or running your own company, the good news is that each of the previous reasons applies, and you don't need to convince anybody but yourself.

So ... what's next?

First things first. Becoming an MVP is a marathon, not a sprint. You need to be truly passionate about your professional growth and sharing knowledge with your community.

So, if you're seeking shortcuts, I'm sorry to disappoint you. This book is not about shortcuts but about fundamental principles and values you must incorporate to sustainably and congruently live an MVP life.

There's no linear process for becoming an MVP either, not from any vendor at this point at least. It's predominantly a subjective process. You depend on getting nominated for the recognition (in general by some other active MVP or internal employee from your vendor) and on different people voting in your favor based on the impact of your community contributions.

You will learn everything about nomination processes in Chapter 5.

However, you must first learn about the philosophy behind community award programs and the key principles you must respect. I'll be covering that for you in the next chapter.

As part of that philosophy, also in the next chapter, there are certain myths I'll be debunking as well as common pitfalls you can avoid.

In Chapter 3, you'll learn about the four strategic pillars that will serve as your foundation to tailor how you plan to contribute and positively impact your community.

In Chapter 4, I walk you through some concrete steps that you'll find very valuable to support your MVP journey. By consistently applying them, you should have a better chance to succeed in your goal of becoming an MVP for the first time or to get a renewal.

I applied these principles and strategies for myself and the MVP aspirants I have coached, whom after following some of these ideas have achieved their MVP status.

Now, I'm sharing it all with you in this book. I hope you find it useful and helpful to thrive in your career and life.

Last, but not least, in Chapter 6, you'll learn how to make the most of your MVP powers once you get awarded, putting them at the service of your community.

This book is designed to put the lessons you learn into action and consciously move you toward your MVP designation.

Wherever you find a *Take Action!* section in the upcoming pages, it means that you have an opportunity to make real progress. After helping you reflect on some fundamental questions and beliefs behind your MVP aspirations, those sections will help you tailor your strategy to support your MVP goals and become a better you.

2 YOUR PHILOSOPHY

"The greatest among you will be your servant."

Matthew 23:11

Becoming an MVP is not for everyone but may be right for you. It requires a true passion for your technology or the product you work with every day, true determination to take your professional career to a higher level, and a profound desire to make a difference in your community.

You can't be an MVP without deeply incorporating these elements into your daily life, both professionally and personally.

If you want to be successful in your MVP aspirations, you need to respect key principles on your MVP journey, unveil prevalent myths, and avoid common mistakes. This chapter walks you through all of these.

Principles

Forget about the award. If you believe that being an MVP will bring you fame and make you better than others, then you probably won't become one. Or, if you are already an MVP, you may not deserve to hold that status for long.

Being an MVP is about serving others. It's about having a passion for what you do and sharing that passion with your peers in your community. It's about sharing knowledge, respecting others, learning, and growing every day.

It's a way of living your professional life and even your life itself. If you share these principles and have the right attitude, I support you and recommend that you go for it. Being an MVP is an amazing way of life, but only if you're in it for the right reasons.

Is being an MVP for you? If you identify with the basic principles that follow and want to commit to them, then you may be MVP material.

Principle #1: Genuine Community Spirit

You don't become an MVP by being the most prepared and certified professional in your area or by knowing the right people. The only reason for being an MVP is to **serve your community just for the sake of it.**

That's the right attitude and the only sure way to accomplish your MVP aspirations and feel fulfilled.

It's so gratifying to see that what you are doing is truly helping others. It's transformative.

People usually recognize and thank you when you help them.

Something as simple as responding in a forum could significantly save others several hours and headaches. Your impact is even greater if you can deliver some content that solves a broader problem in your community. You can do this through a video, blog post, conference session, or any other form that works for you.

The more positive impact you generate, the more you'll feel fulfilled, and the more you will be modeling the right attitude as an MVP.

So, search your soul. Are you pursuing helping others in your community just for the sake of it or merely going for the award? Do you have the right attitude?

There's nothing bad about achieving the award. The honor is great and fair if you've significantly contributed to your community. Just be clear that the award is a consequence of your burning desire to help others. The award itself is not the driver.

Principle #2: Passion

Passion is the fuel that can power you toward becoming an MVP in your area of expertise.

You'll be spending a lot more time on the journey than you will at the ultimate destination, which is not a destination in itself but actually a door to new amazing opportunities to take your passion to new unthinkable levels. So, if you are not passionate about your technology or product of choice, becoming an MVP will be such a burden for you that you probably will give up trying. Period.

You'll have a lot of costs associated with your MVP journey. For example, plan to spend some nights and weekends serving your community instead of hanging out with your family and friends, invest from your own pocket to attend a conference, or reduce some billable hours.

A true passion for what you are doing to serve your community is what will keep you going.

Look inside and ask yourself whether a product or technology from your vendor really lights you up, resonates with who you are and is something you are passionate about.

You'll be known and associated with that product, technology, solution, or discipline, whichever denomination works best for your specialization. It will be part of your DNA. So, you will want to be in communion with it.

You'll learn more in the next chapter what to consider and how you can make a more calculated choice if you haven't already made yours.

> *"Passion is the fuel that can power you toward becoming an MVP in your area of expertise."*

> **Pablo Peralta**

Principle #3: Desire to Transcend

If you're reading this book, it's probably because you believe you're called to do better than what you are doing now.

You may have a true, burning desire within you to make a difference in your community. That burning desire is your call to transcend, to put your talents and the best version of yourself at the service of your community. It's your call to become a better you.

I recommend that you reflect and determine whether that is a genuine call for growth or your ego seeking public recognition.

If this deep desire to transcend is about contributing your gifts to your community, then keep reading this book. If not, you may want to reconsider the idea of becoming an MVP and incorporating its principles. You may need to make a shift before continuing, or just quitting—and that's also fine. Know that aspiring to become an MVP will be worth doing and will yield amazing payoffs in the future.

Principle #4: Willpower

Your MVP journey won't be free. There's a price you will need to pay—maybe not directly in the form of money but in some tradeoffs, you will need to make to achieve your MVP goals.

So, take a moment and ask yourself whether you're truly willing to pay that price. Reflect on whether you're willing to accept the components of this challenge:

Incorporate good habits and abandon some bad ones in your life.

- Commit to learn and grow every day.

- Openly help others, share knowledge, and seek out opportunities to do so.

- Volunteer to do what others in your field are not willing to do.

- Dare to lead a local user group community; speak at events; contribute through your blog, social media channel, open-source project, or wherever you understand your community has a gap you can fill through your leadership.

- Spend some additional early hours, nights, or weekends, depending on what works best for you, in your technology or product of choice instead of watching TV.

- Become an influencer, more responsible, and conscious about the opinions you express.

- Do it all just because you feel fulfilled when you learn and share with others, without expecting anything in return.

If you are ready to embrace most of the preceding principles, it may indicate that you are truly passionate about what you do and that you have what it takes to embark on your MVP journey. So, continue reading to explore upcoming pieces of advice you should find very useful.

> *"Knowledge is important, but it's not what will take you there. Being an MVP is more about being passionate and serving your community than knowledge."*
>
> **Pablo Peralta**

TAKE ACTION!
YOUR FOUNDATIONAL QUESTIONS

Ask yourself the five foundational questions that follow to find out whether the idea of becoming an MVP truly resonates with you. Choose the one answer that describes you best.

1. Are you passionate about your product or technology?

.... *Yes!* .... *Maybe* .... *No*

2. Are you passionate about sharing knowledge with like-minded people and selflessly helping others, or do you want to become an MVP just for the prize, status, or benefits?

.... *Yes, I am passionate and would do it anyway, regardless of the award!*

.... *I don't dislike sharing my experiences, but wouldn't do it if there were no awards attached.*

.... *To be honest, my main driver is actually the award.*

3. What is your real purpose in becoming an MVP? What is your "why"?

....

....

....

....

4. Are you willing to pay the price?

.... Yes .... No

List some of the costs associated with your MVP journey and verify whether you're willing to pay the price (e.g., postponing watching the hottest new TV series, sacrificing some family time, reducing your billable time, spending some nights and weekends producing content to share with your community, footing the bill to attend more conferences and networking opportunities).

....

....

....

5. Will becoming an MVP make you happy?

.... Yes! .... No

Happiness comes from:

- not just the AWARD but WORKING TOWARD IT as well.

- not only the final destination you intend to reach but also the JOURNEY that leads there. Remember, you'll be spending a lot more time on the JOURNEY than you will at the ultimate destination.

Yes! I am absolutely certain that becoming an MVP will make me HAPPY because . . .

....

....

....

Myths

Okay, so far, so good. Now it's time to debunk some of the myths you may have heard about becoming an MVP.

Myth #1: You Must Be a Guru

Many of the MVPs out there are, no doubt, considered gurus in their field. But, while that makes a lot of sense, it doesn't mean that becoming a member of the MVP family requires such eminence.

I've never been a guru, neither have I felt that way. Actually, during my time as a tech consultant, I used to work with people with much technical knowledge than me but who may lack the interest, discipline, or willpower needed to become MVPs.

As suggested earlier in this chapter, being an MVP is more about being passionate and serving your community than about knowledge.

Depending on your vendor's program and its award categories, sometimes it isn't even required that you have technical skills in its products, but you can also be a business-oriented MVP, evangelizing about its products from a business perspective, not technical.

So, start by contributing from where you are now. Don't underestimate what you already know at this point and what you can learn from exploring and trying to make what you find available to your community, whether it's technical or business-related.

The more curious you are, the better for you and your community. So, light up your curiosity, set yourself apart from the illusion of perfection and knowing everything, and just humbly share what you've discovered about your technology or product.

You'll be amazed at how much positive impact you're able to create through your impulse to share just as you are, just what you know now.

Myth #2: You Must Be a Great Public Speaker

You may know many of the MVPs because they stand up and speak at conferences, attend user group events, deliver webinars, post on YouTube, and have a presence on other public channels.

But the reality is that not all of them are great at speaking. Far from being Steve Jobs on the stage, many MVPs find themselves out of their comfort zone when speaking. Yet, their desire to share their passion is bigger than their fear of public speaking. And that's part of what helps them grow in their careers and gain confidence.

Whenever you share in public what you've learned, it means that you're expanding, you're growing. If you feel the grace of sincere applause from your audience, that's all the better. That applause is powerful. It indicates that you're truly adding value to others; you're becoming an MVP inside and out.

Now, while speaking is a great way to contribute and positively influence others, that doesn't mean you need to go out and step in front of an audience if that freaks you out.

Some MVPs don't do public speaking but greatly contribute through other means. For example, they may share tools or pieces of code with the community, write blog articles or books, and even organize user group events or conferences without being speakers themselves. And all that is fantastic and perfectly resonates with the MVP spirit.

So, consider public speaking as just one of the avenues that you can take on your MVP journey. There are several other avenues and ways that may work better for you and will take you to the same destination.

Myth #3: You Don't Have the Time

Be careful with this myth because this is usually an excuse or fear in disguise.

When I became an MVP for the first time, I was working long hours in consulting projects to feed my family after losing a lot of money in startups that didn't work. I was married and had two children already that demanded my attention. I needed to drive from home to office, which usually took me hours a day. I was traveling like crazy, among other obligations and time-consuming activities. Throughout the years, that didn't stop but increased as more responsibilities arose. We were blessed with a third child. I didn't stop starting up new businesses, and the list is long. So, I didn't look like someone with a lot of free time, right? Neither I do today.

However, it's fair to say that becoming an MVP does require dedication. So, how does it work? Which is the missing piece here? The answer: **it's all about a mindset shift.**

If you understand that the path of the MVP makes you a better professional and person every day and that you truly will have a return on your time invested, getting paid off usually sooner than later for your efforts, you will decipher the code for all of this. Hence, if you're being whipped by the misbelief that you don't have the time to become an MVP, this is an indicator that you still didn't your mindset shift.

The shift implies the understanding that by investing in any MVP-related activity, you're in reality investing in yourself. And that's the best investment you can do in your life. It will expand you to unthinkable levels, both professionally and personally.

There is countless evidence of how this expansion manifests, from the new knowledge that you incorporate, and takes you to new levels of expertise in your career—and as consequence, get better paid. You get more resources that will save you a lot of time, which translates into unquestionable returns on your time investments. You also gain new connections that can earn you unimaginable opportunities, meaningful friendships that last forever, and many more just because you did your mindset shift and were determined to become better.

You can always balance how much of your time you dedicate to learn more and contribute to your community; that might vary over time, but you must create those habits.

I will be elaborating more on this in the next chapter, but for now, I encourage you to look into your current habits and look at opportunities you could harness to incorporate the right ones. You could simply start by spending some few minutes daily in your community forum trying to help others while learning a lot from real-world challenges they are facing in their projects.

However, as important as it is to gradually incorporate new good habits, it's to eliminate the bad ones that won't take you there. Believe me, neither TV shows nor scrolling through social networks will support you.

So, if you still didn't, reflect a little bit and do your mindset shift so you make the best investment you can do in your life which is in YOU. The mindset of the MVP is one of self-growth, expansion, contribution, fulfillment, and gratitude. I haven't seen anyone regretting the time invested in any of these things; they always just pay off.

Myth #4: MVPs Don't Make Mistakes

Being an MVP doesn't mean you're perfect. Far from that! MVPs make mistakes all the time, and good ones recognize and keep learning from them.

Perfection is an illusion. It's your worst enemy, not your mistakes.

On the contrary, making mistakes means that you're experimenting with new things. You're giving yourself space to grow, learn, gain more experience, and receive valuable, constructive feedback from others in your community.

Whenever you're delivering a session or publishing something, live with the imperfection and with the fact that you're just sharing what you know at that moment. There may be many other different points of view, experiences, and ways to do things.

Everybody assumes that what you're sharing is what you know; it's just your viewpoint. Nevertheless, if it makes you feel more comfortable, do make a disclaimer explicit to your audience, especially if you're trying to demonstrate something brand new or unstable that has a great chance of failure.

Don't abuse using these types of disclaimers, though, if you use them properly, they may be a great relief. When others disagree with you, avoid being on the defensive but be graceful and open to incorporate others' points of view and experiences.

Also, plan for a backup if you're delivering a live session. For instance, what will you do if, eventually, your demo fails? Be prepared. Bring with you a video or a series of slides showing how it works so you don't go blank at that moment, unable to share your message or continue your presentation.

The truth is that if you cannot live with mistakes and you act like a perfectionist freak, your MVP journey will be much slower and more difficult.

The MVP journey isn't a race for perfection. It's a goal for those who make things happen and openly share what they know.

Don't wait for just the right time. Don't wait for just the right content. Take action, and do it now.

I used to be one of those perfectionists in the past, and believe me, I'm not proud of it. Thank goodness I abandoned perfection in my life. I'm much happier now, and I can deliver much more to others, even when I know that it's far from perfect, like this book you're reading!

"Done is better than perfect."

Sheryl Sandberg

Myth #5: MVP Is a Certification

Not! MVP isn't a certification on your technology or product. It has nothing do to with studying and taking any official exam. MVP, rather, is an award, a recognition from your vendor because of your contributions to the community.

Thus, whenever you see the MVP designation on someone's profile, listed among his or her official certifications, that's a mistake.

Besides, the MVP award recognition lasts generally 12 months, whereas certifications, once achieved, last for your lifetime. They may become obsolete, as in the case of the Solution Developer certification I got from Microsoft in 2005—remember that one? But anyway, I hold it forever with me among my past accomplishments.

Earning a certification is different than receiving the MVP award. You receive the award for a 12-month or similar period, depending on your vendor. Unless you break a code of conduct, nobody is going to take it away from you during that period. The time frame is set.

No less, no more. You'll need to apply for renewal if you want to continue to be an MVP.

You'll learn much more about what you can do to live an MVP life and keep renewing your trophy once achieved in Chapter 6.

Myth #6: MVPs Make Money From Their Contributions

The essence of being an MVP is to contribute just for the sake of it, not to get any money in return. So, if you ever heard or thought that MVPs receive direct money for their contributions, that's a myth and is false.

Moreover, most vendors will disqualify you for the MVP award if you produce content or help for profit. **MVPs contribute to their communities because of their passion and willingness to help others, not to get rich.**

However, that doesn't mean you can't charge anything at all. If you've got some associated expenses related to your contributions, you may want to get them covered in some way. For example, you may recoup the cost of food and beverages for some community events, workshops, or the fee for using an online broadcasting platform.

Or, if you're creating content that's so high-quality and demands tremendous time or third-party services to get produced, some minimal, reasonable charges would be broadly accepted and expected. For instance, if you're publishing a book like this one, a well-produced compelling course, a toolkit you developed, a website or app with high costs attached, these would be viewed as reasonable associated costs.

A small fee usually serves as insurance, as well, when you've got limited spots, for instance in workshops, and you want to fill the seats with only those truly committed to learning. In those circumstances where a money transaction is involved, ask for only the minimum fee (or just a complimentary donation) and be sure to document and clarify that when you submit your contributions for the MVP award to your vendor. You will learn more about keeping track of your contributions in Chapter 3.

Also, make it clear that you are not doing it for a living but are truly unselfishly serving the community.

Even though money won't come directly from your contributions to your community, the well-known principle of abundance applies to the MVP world: "What you give is what you get."

So, if you're following your passion, becoming an MVP will be so rewarding by itself that you won't care about being compensated for it, even if you need to incur some costs sometimes.

Consider it the best investment ever in your professional career. It will pay off by itself, and if you do things right, your MVP status will yield abundance in multiple ways, such as earning more money in your career. You will learn more about how to get the most out of your MVP benefits after being awarded in Chapter 6.

> *"Don't let the desire to be recognized to become your main driver. Instead, pursue being a better you every day and share your gifts with others. Getting recognized will be just an inevitable consequence."*

> **Pablo Peralta**

TAKE ACTION!
YOUR BELIEFS

There are several myths and misbeliefs around MVPs. Before jumping into the deep end, take some moments to reflect on your personal beliefs about MVPs. Choose the one answer that most closely describes your beliefs.

1. Do you believe MVPs are gurus, and you need to be one before becoming an MVP?

.... *Yes, if I am not a guru, I will never attain the MVP status.*

.... *Maybe, but I will give it a try and learn along the journey.*

.... *No, I don't have to be a guru at all; I just need to share with others what I know and find valuable.*

.... *None of the above. I have a different belief...*

....

2. Do you believe you have to be a great speaker to be an MVP?

.... *Yes, if I can't speak to a large audience, then there's no other way I can become an MVP.*

.... *Yes, speaking would be very helpful, so I'd better improve my presentation skills.*

.... *No, I can contribute in many other forms, and speaking is just one.*

.... *None of the above. I have a different belief...*

....

3. Do you truly understand that by dedicating time to become an MVP, you are actually investing in yourself, and that always pays off?

.... *Yes, I'm absolutely convinced of that!*

.... *Maybe I will try it and see how it goes.*

.... *No, I'm not there yet. I prefer some entertainment instead.*

.... *None of the above. I have a different belief...*

....

4. Did you understand that there is no official exam to become MVP, but it's all about your contributions to the community?

.... Yes, got it!

5. Do you believe that MVPs are synonymous with perfection?

.... *Yes, whenever I attend a session or see any content coming from an MVP, I assume that's perfect stuff.*

.... *While I consider MVPs as a trusted source, I understand they're humans making their best efforts to contribute, and sometimes what they share is not 100% accurate.*

.... *Come on! Nobody is perfect! MVPs are just great, passionate people seeking to contribute and help others through what they know, not making it all perfect.*

.... *None of the above. I have a different belief...*

....

6. Do you believe this MVP thing is about money?

.... *Yes, definitely. Show me the money!*

.... *Maybe. In the end, I expect to raise my hourly rate, salary, or benefits.*

.... *No. I understand that MVP activities are in no way related to making money but to passion.*

.... *I believe in this mantra: "Give the world the best you have, and the best will come back to you."*

.... *None of the above. I have a different belief...*

....

Common pitfalls

Not everyone can become an MVP—otherwise, the designation wouldn't mean anything. If you are truly passionate about becoming an MVP, then go for it! But be smart about it and avoid some common pitfalls.

Pitfall #1: Wrong Attitude

If you are under the illusion that holding a trophy will gain you a higher status and make you better than others, then I'm sorry to disappoint you. Your main driver should not be a boost to your self-esteem, but rather a true desire to contribute to your community.

Remember from the "Principles" section that being an MVP is about serving others, having a passion for what you do, and sharing that passion with others in your community. It's about sharing knowledge, respecting others, learning, and pursuing growth every day.

Getting awarded is a consequence of genuinely and consistently behaving this way. While an award is fantastic (all human beings love and need to be praised!), don't let the recognition become your main driver. If you do, members of your community, as well as your vendor, may realize you're contributing just to be eligible for the award; and, paradoxically, your chances may fade.

Pitfall #2: Overcrowded Category

You must understand your vendor's MVP award structure to make your choice about which technology you want to focus on.

Depending on your vendor, the overall specialization in a single product or technology may represent an award category by itself. Or there may be several products and technologies that add up to a certain award category—as is the case with Microsoft. There may be categories not based on any specific product but business-strategy-related—as it is the case with Sitecore.

Understanding your vendor's MVP award categories is also important if you want to specialize and contribute content about more than one of your vendor's technologies or products. In that case, it's usually smarter (for your MVP goals) that all your contributions roll up to the same award category.

The opportunity window for you might also vary, depending on the category you choose. Some categories may be more opportune than others for those seeking a first-time MVP recognition.

As a rule of thumb, a new award category, or an existing one where your vendor is marketing a new technology or product within it, is much more permeable for new MVP aspirants than an award category that's already established.

That is to say, the opportunity window for being awarded in a new or promoted category is larger than for others. Essentially, you'll be competing with fewer aspirants, and importantly, your vendor needs MVPs evangelizing about its recent launch.

The opposite is also true: The more established the category already is, the harder it is to enter. In this case, the category may be crowded with existing MVPs or even overcrowded, making for stiff competition. As a consequence, your vendor may be weighing the long-time contributions of others against the newbie experiences of new aspirants in that specific category. Hopefully, that's not the case for the category you chose.

So, here's my advice: Be sure you understand your vendor's MVP award categories. Whenever possible, while pursuing your passion, try to take advantage of your vendor's momentum in new areas and make your smart choice.

Pitfall #3: Overlooking the Geography Factor

Related to overcrowded categories, overlooking the number and caliber of MVPs that exist in your geographical area is another common mistake that may mean the difference between getting awarded and not.

Essentially, the more MVPs in your country or region and the higher their caliber, the harder it will be for you to qualify for the award. You'll inevitably be compared with more accomplished professionals, especially the ones in the same award category as yours.

It doesn't mean that you must outperform other renowned MVPs in your region or else you won't be awarded. It just means that you need to do your homework and be aware of how crowded your award category is, particularly in your geographic area. By doing this research, you also open yourself to get inspired by what other amazing professionals are doing near you. Some of them could even turn into your models and future mentors in your journey. You'll learn more about finding your mentors in Chapter 4.

Nonetheless, like it or not, your nomination will also be competing with other nominations from respected professionals in your geographic area. It's similar to politics, where each state or region introduces different levels of competence and opportunities for getting elected.

Geography is also important to your vendor's market expansion strategy. An MVP award nomination from someone in a new market the vendor is interested in developing may carry more weight than one from someone in a market that's already established.

For instance, a vendor based in the United States with a large existing MVP base in that country may be interested in expanding to Europe or Asia, making the latter regions more permeable for new MVP aspirants.

So, do your homework. Conduct a simple search within your vendor's MVP public directory to find out the number as well as identities of the people you'll be (consciously or subconsciously) compared to in your region, especially in your award category.

When getting nominated, and you need to complete your profile, do not try to cheat your vendor by using your company or employer's address information simply because it may be more convenient for the award. Do not do that. It won't work, and you'll be cheating yourself and your community. In the end, it will make you unhappy (not to mention that you probably would have violated some legal terms).

Instead, do your research to get more inspiration. Connect with other great already-awarded professionals who may mentor you. Properly set your challenges and expectations, and make smarter decisions.

Pitfall #4: Premature Nomination

In the case of nominations, several MVP aspirants fail to get awarded because they get nominated—usually by some other MVP friend or even by themselves if their vendor accepts self-nominations— before having enough of a track record of constant community contributions during at least the last 12 months. That number may vary depending on each vendor's program, but it usually represents the minimum period of constant community service you have to demonstrate to be considered for recognition.

If it's your first nomination, I recommend you have at least 24 months of contributions before getting nominated. Remember that becoming an MVP is a marathon, not a sprint. As a rule of thumb, the more prepared, the greater your chances are.

In Chapter 5, you'll learn more about how and when to get nominated, but my general advice is, be aware of the contribution history that your vendor evaluates when receiving your nomination. Getting nominated before that is a fast lane toward frustration.

So, don't take shortcuts; rather, grow yourself first. Consistently share your passion with your community without expecting any immediate reward. Be perseverant and control your anxiety. In the end, you're contributing just because you love sharing value with like-minded people, right?

Pitfall #5: Lack of Self-Discipline

Self-discipline outperforms knowledge and any other shortcut you may be enticed to take. Be self-disciplined along your journey to your goal.

Discipline yourself to achieve constant growth, to passionately serve your community, and to openly share your knowledge; and the day may come when you find yourself becoming an MVP.

You may experience some ups and downs—we all do, and that's also fine. But that should be the exception, not the norm.

Evaluate your current habits. Are they compatible with the MVP life you desire? What changes do you need to accomplish the highest impact on your results?

Commit to winning your mornings. For most people (like me), early mornings work great. No interruptions; your spouse and children are still sleeping. Your brain is fresh. As long as you get enough sleep, mornings can be your best partner for success.

I win my mornings most of the time. Of course, there are some exceptions, being married and having children of different ages. But most of the time, I do. And never before have I felt so energic, healthy, and accomplished. Writing this book is an example of that.

But you can also use nights if that works better for you. When I was younger, I used to do my MVP stuff at night into the wee hours. Over time, nights became unsustainable for me, and my health seriously deteriorated. So, the night doesn't work for me any longer but may work for you.

What about weekends? Can you commit to spending some time over the weekends pursuing your MVP dreams?

You must find the time that works best for you and commit to a routine that guarantees consistency in your community contributions.

As it happens in many aspects of life, lack of self-discipline is the mother of poor performance and repeated failure to achieve your goals. Your MVP goals are not an exception to this rule.

So, shield yourself from this common mistake. Plan your routine, commit to it, and remain disciplined in your quest to become an MVP!

> *"Your level of success is determined by your level of discipline and perseverance."*
>
> **Anonymous**

Pitfall #6: Poor or No Strategy

You may have the passion, the right attitude, the knowledge, the desire for self-growth, and even the discipline, but **if you don't**

execute well, you could end up not being nominated or failing nomination after nomination.

Unfortunately, having a poor strategy—or worse, no strategy at all—is a mistake that some MVP aspirants make. Consequently, they get frustrated during their MVP journey.

As with almost everything in business and life, to get extraordinary results, you need a strategy, and you need to execute that strategy. It doesn't mean you can't be at all flexible, but you need at least some framework to boost your efforts.

It all starts with choosing an MVP award category from your vendor that you're passionate about and desire to get awarded on.

What comes after that, and I constantly see it whenever I coach MVP aspirants, is the genuine question, "What should I do now?" And while there isn't a predefined recipe or plan that guarantees you the MVP recognition, you need a strategy that points you in the direction of becoming relevant and valued in your community.

I am going to share with you the strategy I followed for years, which has proven to work for other MVP aspirants I've been blessed to coach. That strategy consists of four main pillars:

1. Focus.

2. Impact.

3. Commitment.

4. Records.

We'll get deeper into each of the preceding strategic pillars in the next chapter. Continue reading; you are getting closer to the Holy Grail of how to become an MVP and keep it up.

TAKE ACTION!
YOUR CHOICES

If you desire to lift the MVP trophy, you cannot be a generalist. Instead, you must specialize. And your first step toward specialization is choosing the MVP award category from your vendor that you're most passionate about and in which you want to work for your nomination.

1. In which MVP award category do you aspire to be recognized by your vendor?

....

2. I chose it because . . .

.... *it comprises the technology or product I love working with, and I'm committed to learning more every day!*

.... *it's my current area of expertise, so I think it would be easier to get awarded in that category.*

.... *it's the category that represents me more as a business-oriented professional.*

.... *it's the new, shiny, promising hot thing that my vendor has just released and looks like there's a nice opportunity there to stand out.*

.... *A combination of all of the above.*

.... *None of the above. I chose it because . . .*

....

3. There are some considerations and limitations to what you can truly commit to doing. Ask yourself: Do you have a reasonable chance of accomplishing it?

.... Yes! .... No!

How do you know it's achievable?

What makes you certain that your MVP aspirations are realistic?

Do you have a track record that gives you confidence?

Do you know people who have achieved the MVP award in your geographical region and your area of expertise? How many?

How do you compare with them in terms of knowledge and community contributions? Do you feel motivated to match their level, or does that goal seem so out of reach that, in reality, it discourages you?

What about discipline? Are you disciplined enough to commit to constantly grow, learn more about your product or technology of choice, and serve your community for at least a year—or even years—without expecting anything in return?

Will your family and your employer respect and support you on this journey?

4. When I look at my goal to become an MVP, I'm certain it's achievable because . . .

....

....

....

3 YOUR STRATEGY

"Striving for success without hard work is like trying to harvest where you haven't planted."

David Bly

The reason I titled this chapter "Your Strategy" is that in order to manage and structure your community contribution, you will need to craft a strategy that resonates with YOU.

There's no linear process to becoming an MVP, not from any vendor at this time. So, there is no silver bullet here either. You will need to seek what works for you—something you really enjoy.

Remember, you will spend much more time on your journey than at your final destination, so you must enjoy it. But at the same time, you want to feel that you're making real progress on your MVP aspirations. That's why you need to respect some principles, lay out your strategy, and commit to it.

So, even though there is no one-size-fits-all solution here, in this chapter, you're going to learn the four strategic pillars you need to consider when crafting your strategy.

Strategic Pillar #1: Focus

Similar to what happens in almost every professional career, if you want to pursue being an authority, you must specialize. A true specialist radiates professional growth, performs at higher levels, is set apart from generalists, and gains the respect of his or her peers.

A common example is in medicine. If you need surgery, you will prefer to see a surgeon, and the higher that person's success rate, the better. You won't even consider your general practitioner for that. Nobody would.

Specialization does pay off. It works if you want to be hired by customers (in the preceding example, you are the surgeon's customer), and it also works if you want to get nominated for the MVP award.

You cannot be a generalist if you desire to lift the MVP trophy. Instead, you must specialize, and your first step toward specialization is choosing the MVP award category from your vendor that you're passionate about for pursuing a nomination.

Probably, though, that first choice won't be specific enough. Depending on your technology vendor, choosing your award category is still too vague, because each category includes several related technologies and products

Even choosing a specific technology or product might not be enough because it may be comprised of several modules, platforms, or sub-products. Take, for example, what happens with development platforms, operating systems, ERP, and CRM software. Each is a huge world in itself.

Whether you're more technical or business-oriented, you will need to go deeper and laser-focus on a niche you're passionate about. You will need to become specialized in that niche so you can make a difference within that community. Your content contributions will be about the niche you're committed to and working to get specialized in.

Specializing doesn't mean that you can't touch and refer to other complementary or related technologies, modules, sub-products, or platforms. But you will need to choose your primary area of specialization—your laser-focused niche. Sometimes, it's not about getting deeper in your category or technology in itself but in the way you apply that technology in your industry or your methodological approach.

This is one of the most difficult choices you will need to make because focusing is not only about being passionate and pursuing excellence in one discipline. It also requires saying "no" to many other interesting areas and shiny new stuff.

If you haven't decided yet, take your time. This is your first, most critical decision on your MVP journey. Of course, you can change your mind later, but that may entail changing direction, potentially getting known in a new community, gaining trust, and adapting your personal brand to match your new niche.

Strategic Pillar #2: Impact

Being an MVP is about creating a positive impact in your community. In the end, that's why you get awarded—because you are making a difference through your positive impact on others.

To generate high impact, you need to consider three key variables: authenticity, value, and reach.

Authenticity

> *"Your time is limited, so don't waste it living someone else's life."*

Steve Jobs

On your MVP journey, as well as in other areas of your life, to succeed and achieve sustained happiness, it's crucial to be yourself, to be authentic.

You are unique. There is no other you, and that's fantastic! People seek out others who are authentic. The best leaders are genuine and reflect it.

Think about leaders in history or your industry. Consider the memorable Steve Jobs, for instance. He was one of the greatest influencers (if not the greatest) in our modern technology-driven world. Did he achieve that level of influence and impact in the world through copying others? Of course, he didn't. His greatness was apparent in his convictions, his authenticity, his unique style.

So, find your own style. What is it that inspires you, works for you, and that you are eager to give to others? Pursue authenticity.

Don't do the same things as other MVPs in your area are doing. There's no point in copying them. Instead, share something unique that resonates with you, in the format that works for you. Soon you will see how your following starts to flourish.

Your content defines who you are and how much value you provide. Focus on quality over quantity. Make sure your outcomes help people to overcome real challenges, and they will thank you with positive comments, gratitude, sharing your goodness with others, and maybe also joining forces with you to collaborate in your projects.

Value

Some MVP aspirants fail to achieve their goals because they're seeking to contribute to their community the perfect content at the perfect time and on the perfect platform.

I'm an absolute believer that perfection is just an illusion. If you're like I was some years ago, it could be so harmful that it can paralyze you and stop you from sharing your talents with others.

So, by no means should you pursue perfection; instead, pursue value. That's what it's all about. Valuable content, valuable solutions, and valuable pieces of advice are what your community is eager for.

In most cases, it doesn't matter whether the content is formatted attractively. As long as it provides extraordinary value, doesn't contain obvious technical mistakes, and reaches out to the masses (as discussed in the previous topic), people will find a way to consume it, thank you for it, respect you, and deem you an authority in your field.

Before developing any content, any material, ask yourself how valuable it will be for your community. Is it a solution to a real issue or challenge? A compilation of valuable lessons you learned the hard way? A step-by-step guide on how to achieve something? A different, innovative way of implementing your technology or product of choice? A piece of code most people will find useful for their project? Or is it just a re-post of some ephemeral news or existing content? Think about this before presenting content to your community.

Don't be like those who copy and paste Knowledge Base articles or re-post others' articles (unless you're providing value on top of it, e.g., adapting to your region, language, or industry). I made that mistake in my past, and believe me, there is no win there. It may not count toward your MVP award, and that might be seen as if you are pursuing quantity of contributions instead of the quality of them. If you previously found that original piece, why wouldn't others?

So, remember that what matters for your award, your community, your career, and your self-growth is providing actual value to others.

Reach

There is no sense in creating amazing content (e.g., great videos or articles) if nobody or very few people within your community are aware of it.

The number of people you're reaching out to and the professional careers you are generating a positive impact on through your content and contributions are among the first variables those who are evaluating MVP nominations look at.

Your reach can be measured by the number of attendees at your conference session or user group meeting, the number of registrations for your webinars, views of your videos, replies to forum questions, readers of your articles, and the like.

Let's take, for example, the business world. If you've been doing some interesting research and would like to publish a relevant article from your findings, where would you like it to be published to maximize reach? In a new blog that you're creating from scratch or in the *Harvard Business Review*?

So, if you're thinking of starting up your own YouTube channel, blog, podcast, or website to share content, think again whether that's what you truly want to do. That approach may require several months or generally years to take off, develop a decent audience, and create some real impact.

Do you truly want to enter into the business of creating audiences for your content (which is legitimate but might not be your real purpose)? If so, that means you want to get your hands dirty in maintaining platforms, spend time and money in systems, hire people, and invest hundreds of marketing dollars to bring people in. **Or would you prefer to take advantage of existing channels where your audience is already hanging out and is readily accessible to you?**

Leave all that heavy lifting to others so you can focus on your true passion, what you excel in—creating valuable content about your chosen specialization, your laser-focused niche.

Some examples of existing channels with already-developed audiences you may want to take advantage of are:

- User groups

- Meet-ups and other local events

- Conferences (strictly related to your area of expertise)

- Community sites and online forums from your vendor

- Social networks groups

- E-learning platforms (especially those already offering content related to your vendor and/or technology you're passionate about)

- Magazines

- Open-source projects that already took off and are in alignment with what you want to offer to your community

If any of these have a good number of people hanging out there, that's great news for you! You have the audience you want to positively impact waiting for you, with some people already taking care of the heavy lifting. You should start from there instead of starting up new channels. Choose the one(s) that resonate best with you to share your passion, demonstrate your leadership, and contribute your content!

In the event that there aren't well-established channels, but, let's say, there is a local user group that meets infrequently, or meeting attendance is sparse, that could also be your opportunity to set yourself apart and show your leadership. You don't have to start from scratch, and you probably will have the support of your vendor, your user group management organization, systems, and others who will welcome your leadership and fresh ideas to re-energize that community. You will want to be surrounded by people who share your passion, pursue similar ideas about developing the community, have developed connections, and will leverage your efforts to maximize impact.

Strategic Pillar #3: Commitment

"Motivation is what gets you started. Habit is what keeps you going."

Jim Rohn

As you learned in the previous chapter, the lack of self-discipline is one of the common mistakes made by MVP aspirants as well as those who are unable to renew their status.

If you like to start new projects but quickly abandon or pause when things get tough, or you get trapped in daily duties, that will significantly reduce your chances of becoming an MVP or getting renewed.

Being guided by your instincts to speak, write, instruct, lead a user group, start an open-source project, or whatever other community contribution you choose is fantastic, and it's a wonderful step. If you already did it, congratulations! You're one of the few who acted, and acting requires courage.

Now, to truly become an MVP and stay one, committing to regularly contribute to your community is crucial. Make it your priority. Truly commit to that.

It doesn't mean you have to do it every day or that you must spend hours each day. You probably cannot. So, be realistic with your agenda and daily responsibilities, and properly plan ahead so that you can incorporate community contributions as your habit.

When working to meet your MVP goals, it makes no sense to publish a series of articles, deliver a series of tech talks, or start a local user group and then suspend all of it for some months until your daily projects give you some relief. I mean, your community is probably not going to complain if you restart again, but that kind of inconsistency will negatively impact your chances of getting awarded by your vendor.

If you're currently an MVP, you may be familiar with the last-month-before-renewal syndrome. That is, when getting closer to your annual review, you react and try to do in one month what you didn't in the past eleven. Bad news: It may already be too late.

Please, don't misunderstand me. It will be extraordinary for your community to get you back sharing your passion and knowledge. There is no harm in that. I'm just emphasizing that **to achieve your MVP award goals, cultivating the habit of constant contributing to your community is indispensable, and the more quality and value you provide, the better. Never put quantity over quality.** It doesn't make any sense.

You may devote some time every morning or evening, maybe a few hours during weekends, or part of your lunchtime; do whatever works best for you. Plan for it. Commit to it. I have tried several strategies and have made changes over time. There's no recipe; you will need to explore what works best for you in your context.

Some days or weekends, you may have other commitments; and that's perfectly fine. You shouldn't feel guilty about that. But those are exceptions, not the rule. **From now on, your new rule is to make the act of contributing to your community a habit!**

Strategic Pillar #4: Records

Being a great contributor in your community, while necessary, is not enough for becoming an MVP or getting renewed. You also need to prove it.

This is why keeping records of ALL your contributions and their positive impact is as crucial as the act of contributing.

Believe it or not, the lack of good records of contributions is sadly one of the most common reasons why some of those who deserve being awarded (or renewed) as MVPs just don't make it.

Keeping a log of your contributions is also a mandatory habit you need to incorporate on your MVP journey. If you begin filling in your records when someone nominates you for the MVP award or, as mentioned previously, when your "last 30 days before renewal" countdown starts, that means that you've missed the magic piece of your MVP puzzle: your accurate records that serve as evidence of your positive impact.

Accurate records encompass quantity as well as quality. Quantity means you don't leave out any contributions. Make sure that you're including every user group event you helped to organize or you spoke at, every session you delivered at a conference or webinar, workshops you facilitated, articles you wrote, community forums you contributed to, open-source projects you developed, and the like. On the other hand, quality means you include as much evidence as possible, especially URLs and stats that make it easier for your vendor's evaluators to realize how valuable your contributions were for the community.

I recommend you save URLs and pics of social posts as additional backup proof of some important contributions, especially those where the original URL may expire within a few weeks or months, or where website content is subject to change. Take conferences as an example. After a conference is over, its website usually is updated; when content for the next conference is up, odds are the session you delivered last time is no longer listed anywhere. Thus, hold onto some backup proof.

If accessing your content requires getting authenticated for a website or platform (e.g., by username and password), make it easy for your vendor by providing in your records a valid credential or by pointing to information on how to get one. This limited access is sometimes the case if your content is stored on a technology platform managed by a third party, in conference recordings, or behind a restricted LMS (Learning Management System), or similar situation. Be sure to clarify that your contributions are still free of charge, but accessing them just required authentication.

Last but not least, do not brag or exaggerate anything in your records. Those practices aren't aligned with the values of a community leader. Believe me, those reviewing your records are very smart and have highly trained eyes to quickly identify questionable entries.

So, how can you keep accurate records? There are several ways. It all depends on your current situation, your vendor's system, and what works best for you. What follows are the recommended ways that worked for me.

Log It Right Away (or Even Before It Happens!)

Whatever system you use (your vendor's MVP website, your custom Spreadsheet, a document, sticky notes, or a piece of paper), a couple of minutes now will save you tremendous time and effort later—when you must submit your records to your vendor upon being nominated as a new MVP or evaluated to get renewed.

Scrambling to document your contributions is a kind of stress you easily can avoid, and it feels so good to see your list of contributions grow! Immediately after sharing some valuable content with your community, logging your contribution is the best thing you can do.

I would even suggest logging it before your actual contribution happens. For instance, let's say you are committed to delivering a session at a conference, webinar, or user group meeting. Most likely, the event is already listed on a website. Well, just after it's listed and before it happens, include it in your records. Similarly, if you're posting an article, schedule it for a few minutes in the future, copy the link location, and include it as part of your MVP records before it's even posted.

This way, you not only avoid forgetting to do so, but you can also enjoy the grace of visualization. It's magic!

Just be aware that when submitting your contributions, your vendor will consider only what you contributed in the previous 12 months (or another specified period), not any future promises. Still, logging the event in advance could be a helpful practice for your record-keeping.

Log It Directly on Your Vendor's MVP Website

Microsoft is an example of a technology vendor that provides a web platform for MVP nominees and current MVPs to fill in their profile and track online all their community contributions and their impact. Some contributions (i.e., participating in meetings with the product teams) are even logged automatically for you, which is wonderful!

Despite signing into a web system and clicking a few times, usually, it's not as fast as opening a Spreadsheet or note-taking app, in the end, it's the official log where your contributions should be listed to be considered for the award. Thus, by using your vendor's platform, it means you already are a step closer to your first-time recognition or renewal. Bookmark it and leverage it to demonstrate the positive impact you're generating in the community!

If your vendor does not offer a logging system, or the system isn't available until you are nominated, continue reading to explore other tracking alternatives.

Use Your Custom Log

If you are an MVP aspirant who has already started contributing to your community, but you don't have a formal tracking system for your contributions, I strongly recommend you start today. Not tomorrow; I mean today!

By procrastinating this, you're giving to the universe a signal that becoming an MVP is not so relevant to you, or you doubt of yourself. It's fear and worry in disguise. It won't work. Instead, make becoming an MVP your determination and commit to the habits that will take you there.

As you have already learned in this chapter, keeping track of your contributions is a habit you must incorporate and cultivate on your MVP journey.

If you haven't been nominated, you likely won't be able to enter your vendor's MVP website to fill in your profile and upload your contributions. But that doesn't mean you can't keep your own records. Far from it. You should have them all in one place so that when your nomination occurs and you need to enter the data on your vendor's platform, you just need to do some simple copy-and-paste work.

Believe me, copy-pasting is so much easier than trusting your memory to recall all the volunteering activities and great content you've been sharing in the last 12 months. Sometimes I can't even remember what I did 12 hours ago!

I recommend using a simple spreadsheet to keep track of your contributions. This method does a great job and doesn't require much work. For each contribution, just make sure you include the following items:

- Title of your activity (e.g., the title of your session, blog post article, forum, or user group in which you are contributing)

- Primary technology/product (This should be your field of expertise 100% of the time. Remember: focus on your niche!)

- Status (e.g., published, posted, in progress)

- Publish date (i.e., the actual or scheduled date)

- Contribution type (e.g., user group meeting, organization, blog, forum, conference, open-source project)

- Link to activity (i.e., the URL of your published article, video, user group meeting, session or even pics or social posts—where actual proof of your contribution is located)

- Impact (some measure of the positive impact you generated through your activity, e.g., number of attendees at your user group session or webinar, number of views of your video or article—which you may need to fill in after the event)

Note: You are welcome to try the MVP Log & Planner spreadsheet I've created for you to start tracking your contributions. You can download it free of charge from here: **https://www.becomemvp.com**

Leverage Productivity Tools

Maybe none of the preceding techniques works for you. No worries; you still have another alternative. This technique won't avoid some necessary compilation work in the future but will save a significant amount of time while making sure you aren't missing any important contribution you've brought to your community.

That alternative is to use a productivity tool that easily allows bookmarking websites and articles, taking notes, and capturing screenshots from any device—whether you are connected or offline. Examples are Evernote and OneNote, but there are other similar tools.

When you've been nominated or want to get renewed, you need to submit your contributions to your vendor's web platform or similar online site. At that time, at least you will have it all tracked, won't need to trust your memory, and chances are, won't leave out any of your great contributions.

TAKE ACTION!
YOUR STRATEGY

1. Focus.

You have chosen your MVP award category. That's good. Now let's go deeper.

Following are some ideas that may help you laser focus:

- Which specific sub-product/module/business area or variant from your technology or product of choice do you plan to be known for?

- Is there any sub-area that other MVPs are not addressing much that could be an inspiring opportunity for you to differentiate yourself?

- Does that sub-area inspire you so much that you will want to blend it with your identity?

- Are there other methods of using or implementing your product or technology of choice that others are not talking about?

- Do you need more time to think about it and perhaps try some options to discover the best niche for your journey?

- Which other shiny things are you going to say "no" to or at least relegate to a secondary place for now so that you can stay laser-focused on your niche? Are you willing to do that? How do you feel about that level of specialization?

I want to laser-focus and be known as an authority in . . .

....

....

2. Impact.

Remember, there are three key variables that will be considered in the evaluation of your contributions:

Authenticity: Find your own style, discover your "you," what really inspires you, what works for you. Be eager to give to others in your own authentic way.

Value: By no means pursue perfection; it's value you're after. Valuable content, valuable solutions, and valuable advice are what your community is eager for.

Reach: There is no sense in creating amazing content if nobody or very few people in your community are aware of it.

So, take a moment to explore and think about where you're going to share your unique wisdom, goodness, and value. It should be a place that maximizes the number of people who will benefit from it.

1. Is there any local community or user group you can join?

.... Yes .... No

If you answered "Yes," list those you find most relevant to you.

....

....

If you answered "No," it may be your opportunity to initiate a community or group. Is there any user group organization that can leverage your efforts?

.... *Yes! I want to start a local movement . . . and I found these organizations that may be of some help:*

....

....

.... *and these friends who would be great people to co-lead with me:*

....

....

.... *No, not applicable.*

.... *Not sure; I'll need to explore this further.*

List how you plan to find out the answer (e.g., maybe you need to ask somebody else or do more research). Be sure to capture your next action.

....

....

2. Are there any online forums to which you can contribute?

.... *Yes* .... *No*

If your answer is "Yes," then list no more than three active forums where you're already contributing or would like to contribute more.

....

....

3. Is there a lack of forums, content, or resources in your local language that you would like to have?

.... Yes .... No

If your answer is "Yes," then outline some ideas about the types of forums and resources you would love to have and what you can do to get started.

....

....

4. Do you like . . .

.... writing articles, white papers, or even books?

.... speaking at events?

.... coding?

.... podcasting?

.... producing videos or webinars?

.... creating other ways of contribution? (Specify)

....

5. How do you plan to differentiate yourself from others who are already actively contributing in your same area?

Consider the following before you answer:

- *What will make your contributions unique? What type of authentic experiences or ideas would you like to share?*

- *Take a moment to think of the type of wisdom and contributions that you (and maybe only you) can provide to your community that others can't.*

....

....

....

6. Will your contributions . . .

.... *solve real problems?*

.... *save many people much time and effort?*

.... *prevent others from making some terrible mistakes?*

.... *provide prescriptive guidance on the right way of doing things?*

.... *represent a completely different approach toward how to make use of your vendor's product or technology (not more of the same when compared to what others are already sharing)?*

.... *be "more of the same" when compared to what others are already sharing?*

7. Which type of contributions will you focus on, be known for, and why?

....

....

3. Commitment.

Think about your daily routine—about how you spend your time during your workdays, evenings, and weekends. Think about your professional duties, your family, your health, and how balanced or unbalanced you consider your life to be at this point.

What time do you usually get up? Is it feasible for you to get up a bit earlier?

How much time are you wasting watching TV, video gaming, social networking, or doing other things that are distracting you from more meaningful goals?

To become an MVP and stay relevant, it boils down to commit to contributing to your community regularly.

So, first off, create a **"STOP DOING" list.** What things do you plan to eliminate from your plate or minimize to make space for something more meaningful like becoming an MVP?

1. ....

2. ....

3. ....

4. ....

5. ....

6. ....

7. ....

8. ....

9. ....

10. ....

Now, think of the **NEW HABITS** you plan to commit to and how you plan to do it.

1. ....

2. ....

3. ....

4. ....

5. ....

6. ....

7. ....

8. ....

9. ....

10. ....

4. Records.

Keeping track of your contributions is a mandatory habit you need to incorporate on your MVP journey.

The lack of good records of community contributions is sadly one of the top reasons why some people who deserve to be recognized (or renewed) as MVPs just don't make it.

> *How will you make sure you can prove how much impact you created within your community when you get nominated (or want to get renewed)?*

.... *I'll track my contributions directly on my technology vendor's platform because I already have access to it (usually the case for current MVPs).*

.... *I'll download the MVP Log & Planner Spreadsheet described in this book (free of charge) from here:* **https://www.becomemvp.com**

.... *I'll use my custom spreadsheet to keep my records well-organized.*

.... *I'll leverage a productivity tool—like Evernote or OneNote—so I don't lose track of what I'm doing.*

.... Other (Specify)

....

4 YOUR JOURNEY

"Every journey begins with a single step."

Lao Tzu

As I mentioned in the introduction to this book, there's no straightforward process you can follow to get awarded as an MVP, at least not from any technology vendor at this time. There's a mantle of subjectivism that envelopes recognitions, which depend on nominations and votes among other factors.

Wherever you are on your MVP journey, consider the 8 steps provided in this chapter as a reference, as a range of tactics you can take to qualify for an MVP nomination.

You don't need to follow all the steps in the same order, except maybe Step #1 (Be present where people need you), because nothing will happen until you find those you want to serve through your contributions. But that's all.

So, fasten your seatbelts. Your MVP journey is about to begin.

Step #1: Be Present Where People Need You

You may say, "I'm already connected with many people in my field. I have tons of friends in my social networks." And if so, that's great; it's a wonderful start! But not enough.

What I mean here is to not just connect with those like-minded people you already know and who in general have a level of expertise similar to yours. Instead, try getting connected with those you're yet to know, those who may be starting in your same area of expertise and are eager to be educated, guided, helped, and served by someone of your caliber.

I reinforced at the very beginning of this book that being an MVP is about serving others, right? **So, first off, find and be present on the spaces where those you want to serve are hanging out today, both online and offline.**

The more people you get exposed to, the more opportunities you will have to share your passion, contribute, generate impact, gain new followers and supporters, and surround yourself with positive energy to persevere on your journey.

So, ask yourself where those you want to impact are interacting and seeking answers to overcome their challenges. The most common places are:

- Local user groups and meet-ups

- Conferences and events

- Online forums

- Groups in social networks

As you learned in Chapter 3, your reach is extremely important when trying to create a positive impact on your community.

So, **make efforts to be present wherever people need you.** Both offline and online. Become part of great spaces where you can share your passion and your great value.

Those spaces may not be the perfect match for you, but if a good number of people who are interested in learning from you are already there, that would be enough of a reason to start there.

If any spaces are still under development (e.g., a forum or local user group with low activity), those also may provide amazing opportunities for you to volunteer and help to make those spaces thrive—as described in the next step—without having to start new spaces from scratch, or maybe you endeavor to do so.

Step #2: Volunteer

If you're reading this book, odds are that you may already have volunteered somehow in your community, perhaps sometime in the past, or you're planning to begin.

Whatever your starting point is, congratulations! Becoming a volunteer in your community is immensely fulfilling and a fast lane toward your MVP aspirations.

Volunteering, generally in your same area or region, is about raising your hand to offer some help to improve your community's experience.

If there are some established groups, you can start by connecting with the leaders of those groups. It's very easy in today's world; they're likely to be highly visible in offline events and online spaces. Tell them that you want to serve, to contribute to your community; tell and ask them how you can help.

You never know how valuable that connection, that hand-raise, can be for your career. And in today's world, that process is free and instantaneous!

Maybe you could be helping to moderate a forum, speaking at an event, being one of the organizers of your next local user group event, helping to coordinate a meet-up, recruiting other potential speakers, or being part of a conference programming committee.

You also could be helping with some logistics, setting up an after-conference social event, perform some social media, graphic art, or similar. The list is endless. The key thing here is raising your hand, making yourself visible, and open to volunteering.

In case there aren't any established groups near you, do not hesitate in reaching out to your Community Program Manager in your vendor—as described later in this chapter—and any official user group organization to find the orientation and support you need to spark the flame of community in your area!

Volunteering is a triple-effect opportunity you don't want to miss. First, it serves and improves your community. Second, by actively volunteering, you improve your leadership skills—those same skills you may have tried many times to gain through books and educational programs. **Volunteering is leadership in action.** Third, as you should have guessed, it's part of what it takes to be an MVP; it's fulfilling and aligns with your goals.

There's one more thing about volunteering that makes it even more fascinating. Volunteering exponentially expands your network. And your network is one of the most important assets in your career and your life.

So, seek out the next opportunity to help your community get together and grow. If there isn't any local user group event or meet-up near you, propose one. Connect with other leaders, potential co-leaders, influencers, official user groups, and of course, your Community Program Manager from your vendor in your area. Raise your hand. Practice volunteering. Chances are, you'll never regret it.

Step #3: Contribute content

There's a well-known saying that "content is king." And it actually is. It's what distinguishes you from others in your field. It's what differentiates the masses (those who just consume content) from the few who create it. It's what makes the top contributors MVPs.

Volunteering and contributing content work together and complement each other for the sake of your community and your MVP aspirations. By volunteering, you're amplifying yourself and everything around you; you're leading and making things happen in your community, usually offline. **By contributing content, you're sharing concrete valuable information, helping others, and putting solutions on the table while demonstrating your passion and knowledge within your MVP technology award category.**

By contributing, you set yourself apart; you become part of the solution, helping to solve the problem.

As discussed in Chapter 2, in the section about myths, contributing your content doesn't require you to be a keynote speaker neither a tech guru—you could be more business than technical-oriented. It's not about knowledge in an abstract way, but sharing your authentic value. It just requires courage, determination, and discipline, as you learned in the last part of Chapter 2.

So, how can you contribute? Well, there's no single answer because it depends on several factors, such as the opportunities available in your area of expertise, your current skill set, what you enjoy, if you prefer coding behind the scenes or jump onto offline or online stages, and how comfortable you are putting yourself out there at this point in your career. The most typical starting points are:

- Delivering a series of webinars

- Showcasing some cool stuff at your upcoming local community or user group event

- Submitting a proposal to speak at a conference you plan to attend

- Recording a brief course or series of videos

- Sharing articles for your community blog or magazine

- Contributing to some open-source project

- Sharing a solution (maybe a piece of code, script, or just a series of steps) to overcome some challenges

- Answering questions in online forums

- Leading a series of interviews or podcasts

You must remember that the more reach and impact you can make through your contributions, the better it is for your community and your MVP goals. So, try to create as much impact as possible with your contributions (refer to Chapter 3 for more on this).

Also, try to get rid of any roadblocks. Believe me, you will encounter plenty of them on your MVP journey. That's why **it's preferable to start sharing content in spaces where you don't need to worry about infrastructure issues or how to bring in audiences; instead, leverage existing platforms for all of that.** User group management organizations and established online communities or open-source projects may be good starting points for you.

But if you need to make some choices (because you may not be sure which platform is best for sharing your contributions), don't hesitate. Starting is more important; so do it in whatever forum, whatever channel. Start. Kick it off. You'll find out what works best for you along the way, but nothing happens until you click the "publish" button somewhere.

Step #4: Find your mentors

Learning from mentors is important in your life and your career, as well as on your journey to become an MVP. Luckily, in today's connected world, mentors abound and are willing to pass down their experiences to others.

On your MVP journey, you should seek and choose a handful of current MVPs to learn from and model some of their best practices.

They already accomplished the endeavors you're getting into and usually have the information you may not yet have access to. So, by gleaning from their wisdom, you will be able to avoid some mistakes and get faster results.

Just a quick alert: Remember, you must preserve your authenticity. By tapping others' knowledge, modeling them, and applying some of their advice, I'm not saying you should imitate them. Rather, just get exposed to great lessons from the field—lessons that you can incorporate on your journey. Not to mention how powerful it is to get in touch with mentors who can exponentially expand your network.

You may be wondering why current MVPs should agree to spend time mentoring you. Well, good news for you:

- Some MVP programs (like the one from Microsoft) include mentoring other MVP aspirants as a type of contribution toward their award renewal.

- When someone is an MVP, he or she should raise the flag of service, of helping others; and mentoring falls in this category.

- Some MVPs are involved in organizing user group meetings and conferences, so they need help from volunteers like you.

- It doesn't take much of their time, usually just a monthly or every other month call and some e-mails in between.

- Mentoring others is fulfilling and powerful because it helps mentors improve their confidence and self-esteem.

So, as you can see, you need not be afraid. Reach out to some MVPs you know or follow on the Internet. Introduce yourself and tell them that you're committed to becoming an MVP and would appreciate their mentorship.

Here are some pieces of advice to guide you when you are seeking a mentor:

- Try to seek more than one (ideally three mentors) so you receive more than one opinion and you're better positioned to getting nominated afterward (the nomination processes are described in the next chapter).

- Find a veteran (if possible, one that has been awarded for 6+ consecutive years) and someone who was recently recognized (<2 years).

- Diversify. Choose mentors who are known in contribution areas that are very different from one another (e.g., maybe some of them are known for leading a type of conference, while others are known for initiating an open-source project or some unique online community). This way, you are sure to have different points of view and more opportunities to grow your network and share your contributions.

When you approach your potential mentor, consider these recommendations:

- Before asking for mentorship, I advise you have already built some connections as a follower or expressed some genuine admiration to the person (it must be genuine; if not, why choose that person to be your model?).

- You can prove your commitment to becoming an MVP by pointing the person to your recent contributions and the fact that you're already reading this book.

- Tell the person why you chose him or her to be your mentor. That's powerful and can be your door to a long-term fulfilling relationship. There are multiple MVPs out there, so giving a "why" to your prospective mentor is like giving a reason why that person cannot say "no" to you and should be proud to agree to mentor you.

Step #5: Share feedback and ideas with your vendor

You and your experiences are unique. Chances are that while you're working on your projects, you discover potential ways your technology vendor's product or platform can be improved.

Is there some extraordinary feature that could improve the vendor's technology in a way that wasn't initially thought of, which could open doors to a whole new world of possibilities? It could be improving some specific modules that would allow the vendor to outperform competitors. It could also be some minor adjustment that could save hours of work, or maybe some bugs that need to get fixed.

Is there any preview or beta program from your vendor about some upcoming cool new version or functionality of your product that you could join and contribute with your ideas? If you're allowed to be part (it usually requires to sign off some NDAs and commit to giving feedback), that would be an insuperable opportunity for you to influence the evolution of your product or technology of choice.

In essence, whatever you think can improve the lives of others like you, who are working with the same technology or product, might be an extraordinary opportunity to make one of the greatest contributions you can make for your community: Share it with your vendor!

Most people just don't share feedback when they're invited to, resign to live with the technology as is, or even worse, they later complain alone or in social networks and do nothing about it. But you won't. You're different. You want to truly improve things around you.

Giving honest feedback through your vendor's approved channels not only gives you and your peers the chance to receive what you ask, but it also turns you into someone who raises his or her voice for the benefit of others. That's part of becoming a thought leader and an MVP aspirant.

I also encourage you to reach out to Product Managers and Architects from your vendor who might be present at conferences. That way, you leverage the opportunity to discuss directly with them your product ideas—as well as gaining some visibility and valuable connections that could support your nomination in the future.

It's not at all odd that leadership is a highly praised quality and is considered by your technology vendor when evaluating candidates for an award.

So, as far as giving feedback in a positive, constructive way that will benefit everybody, that's another type of contribution through which you can serve your community and reach your goals as an MVP. And it's almost effortless: It requires just asking!

Depending on your technology vendor and your product, channels may have been developed to submit your ideas and issues. So, you should seek out the correct place to share your feedback. Believe me, it won't be Twitter.

Odds are your vendor has a platform for sharing ideas, with some voting dynamics attached to it or at least an e-mail alias or a 'Share your feedback' text area. Remember from the previous chapter: You must keep accurate records of your contributions. So, **make sure you're doing it in the right place, and you can reference it in your tracking records later** (i.e., save any ticket number you receive, URL where your feedback can be found, or even a screenshot if you don't have any other proof).

Open your wish list now; see where to suggest all those great ideas you already have; do it now! You will be positively impacting your technology vendor and their products, your community, and your everyday work!

I can't tell you how fulfilling it is to see a new feature being released in your product of choice that originated from an idea you submitted. It's something that if you haven't yet experienced yourself, I hope you do at some time in your career. And you can start now—just ask for it!

Step #6: Be YOU the change

"Be the change that you wish to see in the world."

Mahatma Gandhi

What about your local community? Is nothing happening there? No events in your area? No active online forum or enough content in your local language? What tool is missing that could facilitate your projects and those of your peers working with the same technology product or platform? Are you a developer and have the skills to develop it?

Wherever you find a gap, that might be your next fascinating step on your MVP journey: your opportunity to create a change, to lead a movement.

I mean a movement so revealing, exciting, unique, and impactful in your community that you can't wait to start it up and make it thrive. You dream about it; you envision it; you're so passionate about it that you're willing to build it as a service to your community.

As farmer Hoggett from the film *Babe* stated, "Little ideas that tickle and nag and refuse to go away should never be ignored, for in them lie the seeds of destiny."

If you haven't yet found that idea that refuses to go away, or perhaps you did but aren't willing to pursue it, don't worry. Most current MVPs and aspirants don't do it either. Some do it after having been MVPs for a long time. Only those deeply committed to going the extra mile truly transcend and meritoriously become part of the hall of fame in their area of expertise. Maybe you are one of those.

Chances are that if you dare to take leadership and create change, you will end up with something unique that makes you a renowned thought leader in your community. It will be attached to your identity as an authority in your field, and you'll feel proud of it.

In general, if you start something relevant, and you have the perseverance to make it thrive, it completely pays off in the future. But bear in mind that, as happens with most entrepreneurship, chances are that it fails. This happens because, despite your enthusiasm, it doesn't reach as many followers as you thought, or you couldn't dedicate the time it requires, or you couldn't keep your enthusiasm up, or whatever other reason.

That's why I did not include this step at the beginning of your journey. Not because it isn't relevant—it actually is. Not because I don't encourage you to go for it—I certainly do! It's just because unless you already started some movement, and it's yielding success, you won't want to put all your faith in it for becoming an MVP.

If you're like most MVPs, you will need first to be present where those you want to serve to are, then start volunteering, sharing your knowledge and experiences through your content, and hanging out frequently with mentors and other leaders that can offer you opportunities to do so.

After all of that, if you find a challenging empty space, dare to fill it through your leadership. Chances are that you'll also gain more attention and supporters for your movement because you'll have become better known, respected, and better connected.

Again, there's no rule here. Sometimes you just need to start by initiating a local user group or providing content in your local language. I did both in my past, and they completely paid off. But, you bet, it wasn't at all easy and took me years.

Others initiated small open-source projects, and after some years of dedication, these turned into essential toolsets in real projects, with thousands of downloads and tens of contributors worldwide improving them every day. You may be familiar with some of these examples.

So, it's up to you. The good news is that there are usually gaps to fill. Go the extra mile and grab an opportunity to be YOU the change you would like to see in your community.

> *"Only those deeply committed to going the extra mile truly transcend and meritoriously become part of the hall of fame in their area of expertise."*

Pablo Peralta

Step #7: Connect with your Community Program Manager

You may be already connected with some representatives from your vendor in your area. If not, you should; they must know about your enthusiasm for its products and community leadership. If you may also get connected with some Product folks, that's awesome!

Now, there's someone else you must ensure to connect to in your vendor and that is the person dedicated to recruiting and building new MVPs in your region or country. It's part of your mission to find and start hanging out with him or her.

You may find that person under the title Community Program Manager (CPM) within the Microsoft space, Program Manager, Head of Community Programs, and similar in the case of other vendors. Titles may vary over time, but in the end, it's your vendor's internal person who manages the program within your area or region.

Maybe there's no specific person from your vendor in your area or region, but their community programs are managed only from their headquarters.

Your mentors will be able to point you in the right direction. They should know who the right representative is or point you to someone who does.

You may be wondering why the Community Program Manager would be interested in answering your messages. It's quite simple: it's part of his or her job, and getting to know passionate people like you about the community would excite him or her.

Besides, by approaching the Program Manager, you're contributing to his or her goals, so you're saving that person time and effort.

You're the shortcut to the Program Manager's success, so he or she will respond to you.

By being on his or her radar, you gain some unique benefits, such as the following:

- You're now visible; you're known and no longer a stranger when your nomination falls into his or her inbox—you'll learn more about nominations in the next chapter.

- You'll be able to receive valuable firsthand guidance and important aspects of your vendor's MVP program that could not be on their website.

- You'd gain better insights and tailored advice to find out the best combination of focuses, activities, and contributions that works best for you.

- You could unveil amazing opportunities where to contribute. Because those opportunities are managed or at least supported by your vendor, you make sure your contributions will create a great impact among the community and, in turn, great exposure for you as well.

- It's always better asking rather than assuming things, and you won't find people managing communities that will not want to talk to you and answer your questions.

So, seek out and connect with your vendor's Community Program Manager now. And when connected, or if you already are, take the opportunity to hang out and say, "Hi, I'm here. This is what I am doing for the community. How can I better serve it?" This is powerful.

Try to periodically meet or e-meet with him or her. It will be highly beneficial to both you and your vendor, and it will be a shortcut on your MVP journey!

Depending on your MVP program, chances are, your Program Manager not only articulates the program in your area but could also be a key influencer, have a vote on your nomination or renewal process, or is the only one who can put you in the door. Thus, being visible and close to that person is valuable to you.

Step #8: Keep up contributing and be patient

Assuming you're consistently and passionately contributing to your community—and your vendor accepts nominations for the MVP award like the majority do—you may be asking, "How long should I have to wait until getting nominated?".

The short answer commonly is: "a minimum of 12 months." –though make sure to double-check if that's also the case with your vendor's program–.

Nevertheless, I would encourage you to first check within YOU where that question is coming from. If it's coming from your inner need to plan and to experience a sense of certainty, that may be fine; it's natural. Do not feel guilty about it; you're human.

But if your question comes from the feeling that the journey is so difficult for you, and you realize you may be doing it just for the award, that may be an indicator that becoming an MVP is not for you. That's also fine. Maybe you are not ready for it yet; maybe it's not your passion, or you chose the wrong award category or product from your vendor. Or maybe it's a combination of these reasons or other reasons that are holding you back. Or maybe you're experiencing some ups and downs. That's also normal; so, please, don't be too critical of yourself.

Just be aware that leading initiatives and community events are not for everybody. There's no sense in all of us becoming leaders because, in the end, leaders need followers!

So, maybe you're okay following, and you're reading this book now just to find out whether that's what you want to do, at least for now; that's great as well. Congratulations! You've taken a minute to reflect and think about your career and your future, and to make some decisions. Most people fail to do that. So, again, I congratulate you.

Now, if you're truly passionate about your product or technology from your vendor, you're committed to growing personally and professionally every day, you love sharing knowledge with others, you have a genuine desire to serve your community, and you're doing what it takes, odds are, you will be nominated (or included in some private list of candidates for the award) sooner or later.

Let's put it this way: If you eat healthily and do your exercises every day, under normal circumstances, sooner or later, you will be in good shape, feeling healthy. Right? This same rule applies to your MVP nomination, whatever your vendor's process is.

So, keep up contributing and be patient! You're getting closer and you will learn much more about how nominations work in the next chapter.

TAKE ACTION!
YOUR JOURNEY

Build and enjoy your MVP journey!

1. Be present where people need you.

> **1. Have you already joined the most relevant spaces (both offline and online) where those you want to serve are hanging out today? That includes official user groups, your local community private group, your vendor's forum, groups in social networks, meet-up groups, and the like.**

List below the top 5 most populated places where your knowledge, passion, and contributions will be praised.

1. ....

2. ....

3. ....

4. ....

5. ....

> **2. Be sure to join them all and briefly introduce yourself and your ideas for contributions, or—specially in online forums and groups—you can also ask others which challenges they're facing today so you can unfold opportunities to share your wisdom and help others.**

.... Done!

3. ***Do some research about upcoming conferences and events around you that you can join to get exposed to new people with whom you can share new ideas as well as nurture.***

Which upcoming opportunities do you have soon to extend your network?

....

....

....

4. ***Is your plan to start a local/specialized/language-specific community?***

.... Yes .... No

If your answer is "Yes," take a moment to list the primary next steps you plan to take to make it so.

1. ....

2. ....

3. ....

4. ....

5. ....

5. ***Which other actions do you plan to take in order to maximize your reach and opportunities to share your passion?***

- Remember that opportunities come in the form of people.

The more people you're exposed to, the more opportunities you will have.

- Perhaps expanding your reach would require you to create or fine-tune your social profile so it attracts the kinds of people you would like to hang out with. Maybe ask for some introductions to other MVPs you admire. You could also choose to publish something on your social channel or website, or join some private groups.

Take a moment and think about what you can do now to get you exposed to like-minded people.

....

....

....

2. Volunteer.

1. Are you already volunteering in your local community?

.... *Yes* .... *No*

If your answer is "Yes," ensure your Linkedin and other online profiles properly reflect your current volunteer positions.

.... Done!

If your answer is "No," are there any established local leaders you can connect with to raise your hand?

.... *Yes* .... *No*

If your answer is "Yes," list some names of people you plan to immediately contact to offer your help.

....

....

....

....

If your answer is "No," are you willing to be that leader who starts up your local community?

.... Yes .... No

2. Do any of the online communities you belong to have a volunteer profile section you can fill in to say you're willing to serve?

.... Yes .... No

- If you belong to some organized community or official user group, chances are, there's a volunteering section where you can propose to offer your help.

- If so, take a moment to find it and make your submission. It usually takes just a few minutes and could change your career forever.

- If you can't find any, try to reach out to somebody there to get some guidance.

3. What type of volunteer work are you already doing or willing to do?

.... Moderating your community forum

.... *Speaking at your next local community meeting*

.... *Bringing in some cool speaker(s) for your next community event*

.... *Coordinating or helping to coordinate a meet-up*

.... *Participating on a programming committee for a local event/ conference*

.... *Helping with some logistics for a local event/meeting*

.... *Finding sponsors to support your community*

.... *Doing some social campaigns or artwork*

.... *Collaborating at the reception desk at events*

.... *Others (Specify)*

....

4. Now, try to include in your MVP Log & Planner, or whatever system you chose to track your contributions, all recent activities in which you have volunteered as well as those you have committed to do.

.... Done!

3. Contribute content.

Volunteering and contributing content work together and complement each other for the sake of your community and your MVP aspirations. By volunteering, you're expanding yourself and everything around you; you're leading and making things happen in your community, usually offline in your area. By contributing content, you're sharing concrete value, helping others, and proffering solutions to challenges on the table while demonstrating your knowledge and passion about your product or technology of choice. When you differentiate yourself, you become part of the solution, helping to solve the problem.

1. So, how do you plan to contribute your authentic content?

.... *Delivering a series of webinars*

.... *Showcasing some cool stuff at your upcoming user group meeting or community event*

.... *Submitting a proposal to speak at a conference you plan to attend*

.... *Recording a brief course or series of videos*

.... *Sharing a series of articles in your community blog or magazine*

.... *Sharing a solution (maybe a piece of code, script, or just a series of steps) to overcome a common challenge*

.... *Answering questions in an online forum*

.... *Leading a series of interviews or podcasts*

.... *Others (Specify)*

....

2. Which specific topics do you plan to touch?

Recommendation: Think about intersections between your areas of expertise and the areas of opportunities. What are those gaps in your community that you could fill through authentic knowledge or resources?

List the top 5 specific topics you plan to deliver on.

1. ....

2. ....

3. ....

4. ....

3. Which content might produce the best value for your community?

In general, this will determine where you should start. Assuming you're passionate about any of the preceding topics, just choose one (or two at the most) that you understand will provide the best value for your community at present.

The most valuable topic for my community is:

....

....

....

4. Now, make sure to commit yourself to actual delivery by producing a minimal piece. Record it beforehand in your MVP Log & Planner or where you're already tracking your contributions. This will help you visualize how you will feel when done and push you forward.

.... Done!

4. Find your mentors.

On your MVP journey, you should select a handful of current MVPs to learn from and model some of their best practices.

1. Think of some MVPs you truly admire and are your models.

Build a list of no more than 6 of them, if possible. Choose those with some remarkable differences in the way they contribute to their communities or their culture, and the number of years for which they have been awarded.

1. ....

2. ....

3. ....

4. ....

5. ....

6. ....

2. Now, choose 3 names from this list according to how much you truly admire them. Then contact them through the channel you think is most appropriate (e.g., through e-mail or social network).

Tell them the reason you admire them; tell them about your aspirations to become an MVP. If applicable, share with them some important community contributions you've made. Let them know that you're doing your homework by reading this book, and finally, ask them whether they would be willing to meet or e-meet you for a 30-minute mentorship call.

After contacting the 3 individuals, wait 2 weeks. If any of them don't reply by that time, just move to the next person on your list.

1. .... Replied?

.... Yes .... No

2. .... Replied?

.... Yes .... No

3. .... Replied?

.... Yes .... No

5. Share feedback and ideas with your vendor.

1. What is on your wish list for your vendor today that could fix a problem or improve your product or technology? Choose your top 3.

1. ....

2. ....

3. ....

2. Is there any formal channel for the submission of your ideas? (Usually, there is a website with some voting dynamic or online form.)

.... Yes.

.... Maybe, I'll find out.

.... No, there isn't.

.... I don't care at this point.

If your answer is "Yes" or "Maybe," then make sure you arrive at the right place, sign up, and get properly set up to submit your feedback to your vendor.

.... Done!

If your answer is "No," then turn your ideas into a great opportunity to reach out to your Community Program Manager and ask him or her how you can bring your ideas or suggestions to the right team supporting your product or technology. Chances are that you get connected with amazing people who will welcome your ideas and open interesting doors in your career.

> *3. Is there any preview or beta program for some upcoming versions or functionalities of your product or technology you could participate in?*

.... *Yes.*

.... *Maybe, I'll find out.*

.... *No, there isn't.*

.... *I don't care right now.*

6. Be YOU the change.

> *1. Is there some challenging empty space you feel passionate about to fill through your leadership? Are there some ideas that constantly resonate with you, and, in your entrepreneurial spirit, you have a strong desire to make them real?*

.... *Yes (continue below)*

.... *No (skip the rest of the questions under this section)*

2. What does that idea look like?

.... *A local community or user group you want to initiate*

.... *A group that shares content in a specific language or on a specialized topic*

.... *A specific type of content that doesn't exist yet but would be of tremendous value to your community*

.... *An innovative type of event (in person or virtual)*

.... *Maybe development of a tool to make your projects and those of your peers easier*

.... *An ambitious open-source mission*

.... *Other? (Specify)*

....

3. Why do you think this is relevant to your community?

....

....

4. How could you quickly validate your assumptions? Do you need a poll or a quick survey? A couple of phone calls or e-mails? A social media post? A prototype or beta version of something?

....

....

> **5. Why are you so passionate about it? And why do you think you're the right person to lead this endeavor?**

....

....

> **6. Who else should lead this change with you?**

....

....

> **7. What concrete step can you take to kick off and try out your idea?**

....

....

7. Connect with your Community Program Manager.

> **1. Who is the person from your vendor that manages the MVP program in your area?**

....

....

Contact that person. Tell him or her about your MVP aspirations, your recent contributions (if any), and that you're seeking his or her guidance and opportunities to positively impact your community. Ask for a 30-minute meeting or e-meeting with that person.

If you don't know who the Community Program Manager closest to you is, or if the thought of approaching that person freaks you out, don't worry! Just approach any other MVP in your region and ask him or her to help with some introductions.

> **2. Only mark this item as "Done" when you're truly connected with your corresponding Community Program Manager.**

.... Done!

8. Keep up contributing and be patient.

> **1. Are you enjoying contributing to your community? Is it something you would continue doing even if there wasn't an award from your vendor attached?**

.... *Yes, it's my passion!*

.... *Maybe yes, I like it, though I'm also feeling anxious about getting nominated for the award*

.... *No, I'm done. This is turning into a burden, and I'm realizing that I'm doing it just for the recognition*

> **2. How long have you been consistently contributing to your community up to now? By 'consistently,' I mean contributing regularly (x times per week or month) without prolonged interruption.**

....

....

3. When you look at your contributions records—whether you're using your MVP Log & Planner, your vendor's system, your custom spreadsheet, or whatever another tool—what does your guts tell you?

.... *Wow! I'm feeling proud of the impact my contributions are producing!*

.... *Not bad; it looks like I'm making good progress, and I could drive more impact to the community if I just keep up*

.... *Well, to be honest, I'd rather make some fixes if I expect to be considered someday for a nomination*

If you marked the latter as the answer, indicate what you think you need to fix to better impact your community through your contributions:

.... *Frequency you contribute*

.... *Type of content*

.... *Focus*

.... *Authenticity*

.... *Value or Quality*

.... *Actual Reach through the channels you chose to deliver*

.... *Other? (Specify)*

5 YOUR NOMINATION

"Getting nominated is the inevitable consequence of consistently sharing your passion and your knowledge with the community, not the driver."

Pablo Peralta

Microsoft, Oracle, Salesforce, Embarcadero, Sitecore are examples of vendors that work through nominations to evaluate and award community contributors. They usually receive nominations from existing MVPs, internals, and/or customers. Receiving and reviewing nominations is the most usual mechanism through which tech vendors award their top community contributors.

Nevertheless, other vendors (i.e., SAP is one of them) don't grant community awards through regular nominations but mainly through their own recruitment and monitoring of candidates. Thus, you may be already nominated even without knowing it! Or, they provide an e-mail address through which you can ask for getting considered for the award, which may be considered indirectly as a type of self-nomination.

Whatever mechanism your vendor offers to you, if you're an MVP aspirant seeking to get your first-time nomination or being included in that candidate's list, I've got good news for you! That is, if you followed most of the previous steps, chances are that this precious step becomes so natural to you that you won't even need to ask anybody for it.

Getting nominated or being included in your vendor's candidate list for the award means you've put one foot in MVP heaven's door. You aren't fully in yet, but definitely, you're much closer.

The nomination process may vary from vendor to vendor and over time. So, you must ensure that you get the most recent information by visiting your vendor's MVP program website and asking your vendor's Community Program Manager, as suggested in the previous chapter. *Connect with your Community Program Manager.* Remember: it's always better asking rather than assuming things.

In this chapter, you'll learn about the 5 common phases nomination processes consist of according to most vendors and what you need to know before getting nominated.

Phase #1: Meet the requirements.

Assuming you've built your efforts around the strategic pillars you learned in Chapter 3, followed most of the steps in the previous chapter, and did your homework by tracking your contributions, it means that you've properly prepared for this stage, and so you should have a good chance of succeeding. It's like taking an exam—you'd better study and practice ahead of it.

As a general rule, MVP programs consider your last 12 months' performance. So, don't ask someone to nominate you unless you have real proof that you consistently created a positive impact in the community during at least the last 12 months.

I do not encourage you to consider a nomination if you can't boast about at least 24 months of consistent participation in the community. That amount of time further proves your genuine passion, gives you more time to get better known, allows your track record to become more solid, and avoids your being seen as someone who's looking at the calendar to compete for the award.

Think of it this way: If you're truly passionate about your product or technology, and you love community participation, you should be doing it, whether an award exists or not. Right?

So, be patient. As I mentioned earlier, the MVP journey is not a sprint; it's a marathon.

Also, make sure you're aware of the nomination time frames available to you. Just as examples at the moment of this writing, Sitecore allows nominations only in November; evaluations happen in December and January, and announcements are made in February. Salesforce is open for nominations only in November as well, but it announces new awarded and renewed MVPs in march.

Microsoft instead, allows new nominations every month, but renewals are all processed together from April to June, and announcements are made in July.

It's not weird that sometimes new nominations may be closed due to avalanches of them or other reasons, though. This sometimes happens nowadays within the Microsoft MVP program, for instance.

Thus, your key takeaway here is to be clear on your vendor's requirements for accepting nominations and when you can get nominated.

One last thing: do not rush to meet the next nominations period of your vendor. Do not make the mistake of getting a premature nomination, as I described in *Chapter 2*. If you don't feel 100% ready, odds are it's because you aren't yet. Instead, do your homework, keep it up consistently contributing to your community, and get better prepared for a future opportunity.

Phase #2: Get nominated and fill in your application

Assuming you meet all your vendor's requirements, you feel proud of your contributions to your community, and your vendor is accepting nominations, the next natural phase is getting nominated—usually by someone else.

Those who qualify to nominate you also vary from vendor to vendor. You may even be able to submit your self-nomination. Here are some examples at the time of this writing:

- In the case of Microsoft and Sitecore, only an internal employee or another MVP can nominate you. That's, in part, why it's so important that you hang out with good MVP mentors who might nominate you later without your even asking them. It's equally important that you're well-connected with your vendor's closest Community Program Manager, a person who can directly get you in the door.

- Salesforce, on the other hand, requires that an actual customer, existent MVP, or an internal employee nominates you.

- Google requires that an internal employee or an authorized partner nominates you to participate in screening interviews.

- SAP, on the other hand, does not accept nominations in the traditional form but has its own recruitment process and private list of candidates.

- In the case of Oracle's ACE program, you are even allowed to nominate yourself.

Anyway, if your vendor allows you to nominate yourself, I wouldn't recommend it. It's much more genuine if someone else nominates you. Your contributions are considered either way, but there's a huge difference between saying "I'm great, and I deserve recognition" than other key influencers in the community or an insider from your vendor saying, "You're doing awesome, and you deserve the award." It's a completely different scenario.

Whichever the case, if you're actively involved in your community, openly sharing knowledge, giving feedback to your vendor, volunteering and contributing in different ways, actively leading initiatives that positively impact others, and hanging out with the right mentors and your Community Program Manager, chances are that sooner or later, you won't need to ask to get nominated or get in the list of candidates. It will just happen—it'll be inevitable.

In this context, I like it when the results are inevitable. Don't you?

But even if that doesn't happen, make sure you're familiar with your vendor's latest requirements and ask the right people whether they're willing to nominate you based on your track record, your actual performance.

Assuming you were nominated by someone else (as it happens in most of the cases), odds are that your nomination requires your acceptance, and you must fill in your application. This simply means that you supply more information information about yourself and your impact on the community.

That's why, anew, your log is so crucial. Right at this point, you may need to manually enter your contribution records on your vendor's official platform for careful review.

For instance, Microsoft will give you access to its MVP website platform for you to upload your contribution records (a.k.a. your community activities). This process might require you to do some manual copy-and-paste from your MVP Log & Planner, custom spreadsheet, or another tool you chose to keep track of your contributions. Other vendors may let you just attach a file or even bullet list your contributions in a form.

Whatever the case, you definitely would not want to trust your memory at that point. So, maintain your records in a safe place and keep them updated.

Phase #3: Your vendor's review

You've been nominated or somehow you're on the list of candidates under consideration from your vendor for receiving the award of being a top expert and influencer in your area of expertise worldwide. That's huge! Exciting, right?

Well, first off, celebrate it! If you've never reached this point before, know that it's an extraordinary milestone in your career. You've become eligible to receive the MVP award. It's like when an actor or actress gets nominated for an Oscar, except that this is not Hollywood. But it's awesome, anyway!

Be sure, though, to keep your feet on the ground. Getting nominated doesn't guarantee you'll be awarded by them. What it means is that now you're much more visible to them, and your contributions and behaviors as a thought leader will be evaluated.

After filling in your information as requested by your vendor, what else can you do? Well, simply put:

- Keep on doing what took you there.

- Make sure you're enjoying it.

- Be a little more conscious of what you say and do (especially on social networks).

- If you now have access to a web platform or system from your vendor to formally load your community contributions (as is the case with Microsoft), make sure to submit there any new activity that you complete.

- Be patient.

Some—usually very relevant—people inside your vendor will be required to vote on your award. The process usually involves corporate teams and, depending on your vendor's program, it may involve regional teams, your Community Program Manager as well other veteran MVPs.

For example, in the case of the Microsoft MVP program, at the moment of this writing, votes come from your Community Program Manager plus individuals at the corporate level from both business and the product teams. But that, of course, will vary over time and among technology vendors.

In the case of Sitecore, the Community Program Manager doesn't vote but articulates the overall review process. However, their regional teams are also surveyed during the review process to know more about you, especially if you're contributing content in languages those at their headquarters can't understand.

Besides, other current MVPs may also review new nominations—that's the case both of Sitecore and Salesforce at the moment of this writing.

Whatever your vendor's review process is, essentially, the key takeaway here is, you must be careful: "Big Brother is watching you."

The best thing you can do is to keep demonstrating your commitment to improving your community and why you should be awarded among those that are on the same list as you.

How are renewals processed?

The process isn't much different if you're seeking renewal as an existent MVP, except that you don't need to get nominated again but you 'just' go through your annual review phase—i.e., as is the case with Sitecore and Salesforce.

In the case of Microsoft, if you are already on its platform, you just need to keep your records updated there and respect their deadlines so your contributions are considered for your renewal.

Nevertheless, other vendors may require you to submit a new form to get renewed, follow a different process, or no process at all, but you just need to keep being active in the community. This is the case of SAP at the time of this writing.

So, keep an eye on that; make sure to connect with your Community Program Manager and set up your reminders to avoid any omissions in your renewal process.

In any circumstance, however, you must demonstrate why you deserve to earn or keep your MVP status. So, make sure you have contributed and gathered enough proof that supports the fact that you deserve to keep your MVP trophy.

You'll learn more about how to plan for your renewal in the next chapter.

Phase #4: Your vendor's notifications and announcements

You may be asking, "How do I know I have been awarded or my status has been renewed?" That all depends on your vendor's MVP program awarding cadence, and new recognitions may be treated in a different way than renewals.

The most common time frame for receiving some feedback from your vendor is within 90 days after you supplied all the required information to support your award.

Your vendor may use specific months for announcing the award winners. E.g., Sitecore does it in February, Salesforce in March, Microsoft uses July for announcing renewals, and so on.

Whatever the case, you should be the first one to get notified if you got awarded (or not) some hours before your vendor makes their public announcements.

If you don't receive any feedback from your vendor after 90 days, assuming you haven't stopped contributing to your community—and there were any public announcement yet—I would encourage you to check your junk e-mail folder first; and if you can't find anything there, you may want to reach out to your vendor's Community Program Manager. He or she may be able to give you some valuable updates or feedback.

That being said, usually, you will know when you get awarded. And, given it was your heart's desire, you'll experience not only the joy of getting recognized but also the grace of joining a tribe of best-in-class like-minded people.

You will share your passion with them while unlocking a whole new world of opportunities to keep positively impacting your community.

In the next chapter, you'll learn how to make the most out of your new MVP powers.

Phase #5: Celebrate or re-apply later

You couldn't make it this time?

Don't worry! Most new aspirants don't make it their first time out.

The fact that you haven't been awarded yet doesn't mean that you haven't made great contributions or that you don't have enough potential to become an MVP. Far from that!

If you went through a nomination cycle, you're now much more prepared for your next try. You likely have learned a lot about the process, and you've got a track record. You also may have received some feedback (or you can ask your Community Program Manager) about what you need to improve or adjust to having better chances next time.

So, don't consider this a failure. Resilience is part of what makes MVPs. Remember, you're not preparing for a sprint but a marathon.

Some current MVPs I had the pleasure to coach were nominated more than three times with no luck until they discovered what they needed to adjust. And now, they're happy MVPs!

Even though you did not make it your first try, continued perseverance allows you to grow to higher levels, both professionally and as a person.

You may feel a bit disappointed for a while, and that's normal—we're all humans and have dreams. But if you're truly passionate about your product or technology and community sharing, you'll have the resilience needed to recover and get back on track for becoming an MVP.

Make sure you understand where you were lacking in your

contributions, what you missed, what you need to improve upon, or adjust in the way you're contributing or reporting to your vendor. **Was it a matter of not enough contributions? Low impact? Wrong timing? Lack of consistency? Perhaps your MVP award category is very competitive? Did you overlook the geography factor? A combination of the above? Other factors?**

If you still can't fathom the reason you missed out, reach out to your vendor's Community Program Manager to get some valuable feedback about your nomination, suggestions for next steps, and advice on when you should target your next nomination.

Conditions and the time frame to reapply may vary from vendor to vendor and may be different for first-timers than for renewals. So, make sure to set up your new targets properly.

Again, if you're passionate about what you do, which is part of the DNA of MVPs, your continued contributions shouldn't be a burden on you. Continue on the journey that will take you to your MVP goals, no matter when your next chance to become a candidate for the award will be.

So, persevere on your MVP journey! Keep developing yourself, learning about your product or technology, passionately contributing to your community, reaching out to great people, getting more familiar with the process of becoming an MVP, and applying feedback that resonates with your aspirations and who you are.

Did you make it? Celebrate your MVP status and be grateful!

Congratulations! You've got new powers! You're an MVP—one of the top influencers of your product or technology worldwide!

You were so passionate, worked so hard for your community, shared so much value, put forth a tremendous effort, and remained dedicated to your goals. And your technology vendor understood that you're remarkable and deserving of recognition.

First off, celebrate and give thanks to those who accompanied you along this journey toward this unique achievement in your career: your mentors, your vendor, your community, as well as your family and friends. Those are the people around you that encouraged you during this process and also made their sacrifices for you. If you have children, or you're married, or you have a partner, you may understand what I am referring to here.

I encourage you to thank your people both individually and publicly in your social networks.

Sharing social posts is also a powerful way to inspire others to follow your steps. Do not do it for bragging about it but for letting them know that growing yourself every day and serving your community is gratifying and does pay off.

Second, you'll want to make the best use of your new MVP powers. Uncle Ben in the *Spider-Man* series immortalized the phrase, **"With great power comes great responsibility."**

So, let your MVP powers be channeled toward the service of your community, not your ego.

In some ways, you're like a politician that has been elected to represent the people's interests. Your community is made up of your people, and you've been chosen by your vendor to represent it.

Of course, you'll enjoy some unique privileges, but above all, take advantage of the new opportunities to learn more about your product or technology and to connect and contribute to a deeper level.

So, use your new MVP powers for the good and the sake of your community. I'll show you how to do that in the next chapter.

TAKE ACTION!
YOUR NOMINATION

Get to know how to get nominated and how your vendor will review your nomination!

1. Meet the requirements.

1. Do you truly believe you're ready for a nomination?

.... Yes .... No

Do you have a minimum of 12 months of continuous community contributions? Take a look at your tracking records; how much and how frequently have you positively impacted your community?

Try to be as objective as possible and think of why you deserve the award. Do you feel proud of your contributions during this period? Or do you think your nomination may be premature? Trust your guts here as well.

2. Do you have your contribution log updated?

.... Yes .... No

Remember from previous topics, your tracking records are real proof of your impact. At this point on your MVP journey, they're a "must-have" for your nomination to thrive. You'll be asked to provide them, so get them sorted out.

Refer to "4. Accurately log your contributions" in Chapter 3.

3. Do you meet your vendor's latest prerequisites?

.... Yes .... No

Requirements and formalities may vary. So, make sure to visit your vendor's MVP program's website, check every prerequisite and, why not, connect with your Community Program Manager.

2. Get nominated and fill in your application.

1. When is your vendor's next MVP nominations period?

Keep an eye out so you know when your vendor is accepting new nominations. Visit your vendor's MVP program website or ask your vendor's Community Program Manager.

My vendor's next nomination period is on:

....

2. Who can nominate you for the award?

In general, depending on your vendor's MVP program, a current MVP, an internal employee, or a customer has to nominate you.

So, who are those supporters that can put you on your vendor's candidate list for the MVP award? Mark all valid choices.

.... Current MVPs

.... My vendor's Community Program Manager

.... Any FTE of my vendor

.... Customers of my vendor

.... *Anyone in the community*

.... *Myself (self-nomination)*

.... *Other? (Specify)*

....

Remember: even if you can nominate yourself, that's not recommended. Someone else should speak marvelous things about you, not yourself. If you can't find anyone willing to do so, it may be an indicator that you're still not ready, that you still have homework to do for your community before a nomination.

> **3. Now, according to your previous answer, list 3 to 5 valid supporters eligible to nominate you.**

1. ....

2. ....

3. ....

4. ....

5. ....

And of course, contact them and ask whether they would be willing to nominate you. When you contact them, make sure to tell them about your contributions, attach your log, and share related information your vendor requires for your nomination.

> **4. If you've been nominated by someone else or similar, you might be requested to accept your nomination and subsequently**

> *get access to a web platform where you can fill in your professional profile and submit your contributions (a.k.a. your community activities) in the last 12 months in their accepted format.*

So, be sure to have on hand your updated MVP Log & Planner (or another system you used up to now), fill in all required information, and do the necessary copy-and-paste to submit your records as requested by your vendor.

.... Done!

5. If you're already awarded, how does the renewal process work?

.... *I just need to keep my records updated on my vendor's platform (e.g., in the case of Microsoft)*

.... *My vendor has an annual review process, and I might need to prove I deserve to hold the award*

.... *I've got to ask to get nominated again*

.... *I just need to keep active and relevant in the community*

.... *I don't know, so I'd better hurry up and find out!*

.... *Other (Specify)*

....

6. When are renewals reviewed by your vendor?

The time frame for renewals may be different than those for first-time nominations. That's the case, for example, of the Microsoft MVP program.

Other vendors review and process renewals during the same period as they do with first-time nominations.

So, make sure you're fully aware of when you should submit whatever your vendor requires to renew your MVP status.

My renewal period is on:

....

Ensure to respect your vendor's deadlines and retain your contribution tracking records on your vendor's MVP website up-to-date or make sure you submit your data to get renewed when and how your vendor requests it.

.... Done!

3. Your vendor's review

1. You're already nominated (or somehow in your vendor's list of candidates for the award). That's huge! Exciting, right?

So, first off, celebrate it! If it's your first time attaining such height, that's an extraordinary milestone in your career.

.... Done!

2. Understand how your vendor's nominations review process work, when you can expect to get some feedback and how.

.... Done!

3. Keep calm and continue contributing.

Now that you've been nominated, what else can you do? Well, simply put:

- Keep doing what you did that took you there.

- Make sure you're enjoying it.

- Be a little more conscious of what you say and do (especially on social networks).

- If you now have access to a web platform or system from your vendor to formally track your community contributions (as is the case with Microsoft), make sure to submit there any new activity that you complete.

- Be patient.

.... Got it!

4. Your vendor's notifications and announcements

1. *Set up a reminder to an appropriate date to check news about your nomination. Commonly, your vendor's review process could take up to 90 days.*

.... Done!

2. *Make sure to add to your contact's list your vendor's MVP-award official e-mail address (it usually appears on your vendor's website) and/or white list your vendor's domain so you can prevent from their notification falling in your junk e-mail folder.*

.... Done!

5. Celebrate or re-apply later

You couldn't make it this time?

Don't worry! Most of the other first-time aspirants didn't make it on their first try either. That's normal and doesn't mean you haven't made great contributions, or that you don't have enough potential to become an MVP.

So, what can you do now?

1. Be clear about the main 1 to 3 reasons why you didn't make it this time.

.... *The most common reasons are:*

.... *Not enough contributions*

.... *Premature nomination*

.... *Vague technology or product focus*

.... *Low impact, value, or reach of your contributions*

.... *Lack of consistency in the frequency or type of contributions*

.... *Category too competitive or crowded in your area*

.... *Poor records about your contributions*

.... *Others (Specify)*

....

2. Reach out to your Community Program Manager from your vendor.

.... Done!

Be sure you capture his or her feedback about your nomination review, what you missed, and what you need to improve or adjust before reapplying.

....

....

....

....

....

....

3. Plan for your next application.

I can get nominated or re-apply again since (specify the date) . . .

....

To make it next time, I will commit to . . .

1. ....

2. ....

3. ....

4. ....

5. ....

Did you make it? Celebrate your MVP status and be grateful!

4. Celebrate and say thanks privately and publicly to everyone who supported you, contributed to your nomination, and helped you become an MVP!

List the names of people you should thank and share your joy with:

1. .... Thanked .... Privately .... Publicly

2. .... Thanked .... Privately .... Publicly

3. .... Thanked .... Privately .... Publicly

4. .... Thanked .... Privately .... Publicly

5. .... Thanked .... Privately .... Publicly

6. .... Thanked .... Privately .... Publicly

7. .... Thanked .... Privately .... Publicly

8. .... Thanked .... Privately .... Publicly

9. .... Thanked .... Privately .... Publicly

10. .... Thanked .... Privately .... Publicly

5. Put your new MVP powers at the service of your community, not at the service of your ego.

Now that your technology vendor has officially recognized you as an MVP, to honor your status, be sure you commit to at least three main things:

- Take advantage of the new learning and connection opportunities you have.

- Be deeply involved, positively influence others, and do more for your community.

- Keep your feet on the ground and avoid thinking you're better than others.

.... Done!

Don't continue to the next chapter until you have marked this as done.

When you do and are truly committed, get ready for the next fascinating level of your professional career as an MVP!

6   Your MVP Powers

"With great power comes great responsibility."

Uncle Ben, *Spider-Man*

It's true. There's no point denying that as an MVP, you gain more status. Of course, you do! You've been recognized by your technology vendor for your outstanding contributions; you're different.

There's nothing wrong with that as long as you keep your feet on the ground, realize that this status is temporary (generally renewable every 12 months), and that the way you achieved it the first time is and will always be the same going forward: through your passion and community contributions. Period.

So, after the celebration and saying thanks to everybody that encouraged you to become an MVP, the first thing I would recommend you do is to go over the principles you learned in Chapter 2 of this book and reflect on your journey.

Now, get prepared. A deluge of new information will be coming your way—in all different forms—and you'll need to figure out what to do next. The advice in this chapter should be useful for sorting it all out.

Advice #1: Take responsibility

You're now a thought leader in your area of expertise. I don't mean you weren't one before becoming an MVP, but something has significantly changed: You're official now. Your technology vendor has blessed you.

So, whoever hears you speaking at some conference or event or sees your name attached to any publication, content, or social post will know that the information is coming from a recognized source. Some people may even be confused and presume that you're a member of your vendor's staff.

In any case, it will become clear that any opinion you express or information you share in any public space will gain much more attention now. So, be conscious about your new status, behave well, and be a responsible voice.

More than ever, you must preserve integrity as a thought leader. Integrity with yourself, your community, and your vendor. Integrity in the form of what you say, what you do, what you suggest others do, and so forth.

Be aware and also take some time to read and complete the required paperwork. You might need to sign some NDAs (Non-Disclosure Agreements) and other contracts.

So, honor your MVP status; honor your NDAs and other contracts you sign as part of the programs you participate in.

A usual privilege you gain upon becoming an MVP is getting access to preview programs. That means real access to the kitchen. You'll be able to see how new versions or features of your favorite product are being cooked up. You'll be able to smell them, taste them, and even provide feedback that may alter the recipe and consequently the final product that is publicly released.

That's so exhilarating and powerful, but there are responsibilities attached. Unless formally authorized by your vendor, you won't be allowed to disclose what you saw or experimented with. Don't do that even in private meetings. There's no privacy anymore in the 21st century.

I'm not saying that you won't use the classified information you receive to make better decisions in your daily projects. You certainly will, especially when you know upfront that some features or modules will dissipate or experience changes. But that's different from posting about the upcoming changes on social networks or openly sharing information when socializing with others who are not under the same NDA restrictions as you are.

You could lose your MVP status and damage your professional career just with one irresponsible social post or mismanaged temptation to share some exciting news unveiled to you under DNA.

So, behave responsibly as an MVP. Use the information you receive for the good and honor your NDAs!

Advice #2: Do your initial setup and get your MVP Award kit.

If this is your first time becoming an MVP, chances are that you are starting to receive tons of e-mail, invitations, opportunities, stuff to fill in, contracts to sign, and the like. The onboarding process varies depending on your vendor and how mature its MVP program is.

Stay calm. You can't expect to consume and digest in a single day the ocean of new information that comes your way as a new MVP. Indeed, you need to control your anxiety regarding deep-diving into MVP waters. Along with your daily job and family duties, this influx of information can be completely overwhelming.

Permit yourself to go little by little. You've got an entire year (that's the usual timeframe) to find out what it is and the various exciting opportunities you can take advantage of.

Do your initial setup first. Make sure you're ready. Depending on your vendor, upon signing your NDA contract, you may be required to fill in some forms, set up your profile on your vendor's MVP website, join some exclusive mailing list or online group, and so forth.

Don't worry about being overly selective at this point. You still don't know what you're going to receive. So, you may want to start by subscribing to everything, and as time passes, set up your filters so you get only what matters to you.

If your vendor provides a web directory where you can set up your public profile as an MVP, make sure it looks good—meaning it has your picture and as much accurate information about you as possible. Your profile will help other people to find you and will increase your chances of getting invited to speak at cool events and receive more opportunities.

Last but not least, only after completing your initial setup will your vendor have the information required to ship any MVP Award Kit to welcome you as first-time or renewed MVP.

I don't want to spoil the surprises for you, especially if you're receiving the award for the first time. But depending on your technology vendor, you can expect something to put on your desktop or in your library that will be of your pride, among a few other cool souvenirs for MVPs.

Advice #3: Get involved

"Until you conquer the fear of being an outsider, an outsider you will remain."

C. S. Lewis, *"The Inner Ring"*

After finishing up your setup as a new MVP, you will want to get familiar with the new opportunities you have access to. These will take your talents and passion to higher levels.

Even if you're receiving lots of information, you may also want to reach out to your Community Program Manager for the most recent opportunities to get involved.

There will be plenty of opportunities you'll find fascinating and may want to be part of. What comes your way will depend on your vendor and what its MVP program offers.

Some typical opportunities include:

- Participating in exclusive early adoption programs.

- Accessing exclusive resources and subscriptions.

- MVPs-only workshops and early access to certification programs.

- Attending exclusive events for MVPs (e.g., your MVP Summit).

- Benefiting from discounts for MVPs to attend your vendor's conferences and take exams.

- Accessing preferred support from your vendor.

- Having frequent direct interactions with your vendor's product team.

- Submitting feedback and new ideas to your vendor through privileged channels.

- Receiving exclusive invitations to discussion forums.

- Moderating your vendor's community forum.

- Speaking at relevant official conferences from your vendor.

- Leading content creation initiatives and providing feedback about your vendor's product documentation.

Getting involved in most of these will also contribute to growing your list of contributions for your next period's renewal. So, that's fantastic news!

And those are just opportunities that come from your vendor. Now that you're an MVP, opportunities will be flourishing all the time for you

So, I'm happy to share with you some caveats and best practices on how to properly manage them to keep a healthy balance in your life.

Don't have a crisis of belonging

Each MVP is different, but you all belong to this exclusive group. You, like any of the others, are on the same list; you already belong; there's no additional proof required.

Know that what you bring is valuable, as are your opinions. You're not a fraud; you went through the same evaluation process from your vendor that the other MVPs went through.

You're not an outsider but an insider now. You're welcome to join the spaces where your MVP pals are hanging out. So, take advantage of all possible opportunities for you to network with your MVP pals.

Especially, properly budget and plan your schedule for your MVP Summit event and conferences. You get surrounded by so much positive energy, great new like-minded friends from all over the world, and opportunities that I recommend you don't miss out on. You'll never regret it.

Explore first and decide later, with calm

The list of opportunities to learn more and share your passion grows exponentially. However, even though the MVP stuff is so exhilarating, you also might have daily projects to take care of to feed yourself and your family. So, sooner or later, you will need to be selective. You won't have enough time, energy, skills, or even the same passion to pursue all opportunities.

So, you'll need to find out what works for you and keeps you in balance with your daily duties and family life. Each situation is different, and there's no recipe here. But do explore first and then, with more calm, take a moment to decide what you want to get your hands on.

In particular, I encourage you to take advantage of new training opportunities, e-meetings, and stuff that doesn't demand so much time or long-term commitment upfront.

For instance, if compatible with your time zone and agenda, consider participating in direct interactions with your vendor's product team, and submitting new ideas.

Think twice before accepting opportunities that will require a lot of time commitment.

Now that you're an MVP, it's common for other members of the MVP family to welcome you with exciting initiatives for you to be a part of.

Also, be prepared to receive more requests from your local community, current and new followers who write to you, and those who are seeking an expert like you for their events, webinars, blogs, books, podcasts, video interviews, and more.

These might include exclusive invitations from your vendor to authoring a mass of high-quality content, enrolling in some early adoption programs that require a great deal of your time, translating content into another language, organizing relevant events from scratch, leading a new community project, and so forth.

So, make sure you don't overcommit yourself. And, if you decide to get involved in any of these, try focusing on just one at a time. Ignore the others to keep some healthy balance in your life.

Don't get caught in the inner circle trap.

You already belong to the MVP circle; that's a very exclusive circle that most other passionate professionals like you only dream of belonging to. As Charles H. Vogl stated in his book *The Art of Community,*

> *The trap of the inner ring is the spiraling cycle that pulls us from one ring to the next; as soon as we achieve one, we inevitably long for the next, even more exclusive (and thus more attractive) ring beyond it.*

New inner rings can be introduced to you in the form of participating in exclusive opportunities, invitations, events, or new awards (e.g., the Regional Director program from Microsoft or the ACE Director from Oracle).

There's nothing wrong with pursuing more, but do enjoy and be happy where you are now. Go little by little and be sure to keep a healthy balance in your life before even evaluating whether any new ring would be an option for you.

Don't forget what took you to your new MVP status; remember those you were contributing to.

Don't let the shiny lights of new opportunities dazzle you. While allowing them some space, remember to retain your authenticity and the type of contributions you were making before receiving the award, assuming they're still valid and valuable.

Odds are that you'll be excited about new opportunities. It's part of the joy and privileges of becoming an MVP. But, here's the key takeaway: Remember those you were contributing to before getting officially awarded.

Advice #4: Leverage your privileges

You worked hard, very hard. You went the extra mile several times. You've been of inestimable value to your community. You dared to lead and took action when others didn't. You've generated so much positive impact through your contributions. You've sown a lot. Now, it's time for your harvest.

Certainly, just by passionately doing what you do, contributing, and getting recognized, you're already experiencing the fulfillment that pays off by itself. Moreover, if you're already set up and getting involved in new opportunities (I hope you are!), those are amazing privileges you're already getting access to.

But wait, there's even more! Let me share with you some other ways to leverage your privileges as an MVP.

Take advantage of your shortcuts.

Remember, whenever you've got an issue with your product or technology of choice, in addition to formal support channels, you now have a direct relationship with the team in your vendor in charge of it. Even better, you can reach out to the boss or the boss of the boss.

Certainly, do not misuse this resource, but take advantage of this access that will save you and your customers a lot of time and money! Make sure they know that. Believe me, this may be a key differentiator between you and a competitor in a deal.

I experienced that in the past, and it was one of the main reasons an important customer wanted me to get involved in his company's projects.

I seldom had to use that resource, but when needed, it made a complete difference in the project results. And that's a pure value at the bargaining table.

For the potential customer, that access instills confidence, knowing the company is hiring someone who can pick up the phone and reach the right person inside the tech vendor who can solve problems quickly and efficiently.

Get nurtured with invaluable world-class wisdom and connections within your MVP network.

This is your secret weapon, and I would say that one of the main benefits of becoming a member of the MVP family is this: The best-in-class professionals are there.

Your new network has altruistic people who share the same passion and values as you do and are always willing to help you out and offer you their incredible knowledge.

Maybe it's a key architectural decision you need to make in your project and validate against real experiences. Maybe it's a recommendation between one third party product and another. Maybe it's a contact you need in some part of the world or some specific knowledge in an industry or field.

Whatever you need some wisdom on, count on your MVP network. In the same vein, make sure your customers know that by hiring you, they're also getting instant access to the best-in-class knowledge on the planet to solve their problems. That's another reason why they should choose you.

Discover your additional exclusive benefits as an MVP.

These extra benefits—if any—will depend on each vendor's program and may vary over time. They could be in the form of free licenses to use amazing software products, free online subscriptions to great learning tools, pro accounts to platforms for running your meetups and community events, vouchers to take official exams, and so much more.

Check your vendor's website; ask your Community Program Manager and your MVP pals about them. Sometimes these benefits are not very well known, or you need to contact somebody else in the case of special third-party software offers for MVPs.

You may be surprised to find how many related technology and training vendors offer great stuff for MVPs!

Enhance your professional profile.

You're no longer an average professional in your area of expertise. You're an MVP now, and you've been recognized by your vendor as one of its key influencers worldwide.

So, be sure your MVP status is highlighted in your profile on networks like LinkedIn and other professional forums where you have set up your profile. Make it part of your title and e-mail signature.

Whenever there's a discussion, and comment comes from a recognized voice like yours, your opinion will automatically hold more weight just because it includes those three magic letters.

Make it easier for your next customer, partner, employer, or whoever is scanning your profile to realize you're not just average, but outstanding.

Wear your MVP pin and tag yourself at events.

Wear your MVP pin if you received one from your vendor; use stickers and even handwrite on your conference badge to add your MVP designation.

Doing so distinguishes you, is very powerful, and it works. Use it for good, of course.

If you feel skeptical, just give it a try at the next conference you attend by visiting a sponsor's booth with and without your MVP tag. Chances are that you're treated differently because they know you're an authority and an influencer.

Essentially, the happier they make you feel, the better for their business. You will end up collecting even more souvenirs from those booths just by tagging yourself as an MVP. Try it out!

Attach your recognition letter as part of your credentials in every commercial proposal and RFP response.

Microsoft, for instance, lets you download an official recognition letter that makes you stand out. It can be generic ("To Whom It May Concern") or targeted to a specific recipient.

This is a key differentiator when you or your company are competing for a deal. If your vendor doesn't provide you with one to download through their website, ask your Community Program Manager.

If you got the deal for your employer, make sure he or she is aware that your MVP distinction was part of the reason why the customer chose your company over others. That way, your employer will keep supporting you in your path as an MVP.

I know an MVP who also attached his recognition letter for his business visa application as part of his professional credentials! That's powerful! It's a renowned tech vendor endorsing you!

If you're self-employed, it may be a good time to reasonably increase your hourly rate.

No, I didn't forget that! It's just that you need to respect the order of things.

You are more valuable now; you're a recognized professional, influential, deeply connected with your vendor, and the highest talents in your field, so you're saving your customers time and money.

But wait until the right time to raise your rate. First, be great and contribute so much for the sake of it because you're passionate about it. Second, I'm convinced that to keep a balance in this world, whatever divine form you believe in (e.g., God, universe, energy, source), will ensure that you're receiving as much as you're giving.

You're able to produce more than others, so reasonably increasing your hourly rate (especially for new customers and new engagements) will give you more credibility and greater value as a professional.

I would be doubtful of hiring an MVP that costs me the same as any other professional who doesn't have that status. So, increasing your rate to match one that is fair with your new status while remaining competitive in your market will be more congruent and beneficial to everybody!

If you're an employee, try to negotiate some privileges instead of an immediate increase in your salary.

For example, you might ask to be able to dedicate some office hours to MVP activities, ask for a commitment to funding and supporting you to attend your MVP Summit conference or some other relevant conference organized by your vendor, and similar requests.

By maintaining your MVP status and exposure, both you and your employer will benefit.

You can experience a more peaceful life–work and even financial balance by agreeing to some new terms without making your employer think you are directly costing the company more money every month or that you may be leaving the company soon.

Believe me, your employer will be sensing the risk of your departure if you don't set up a time to openly negotiate. Your employer will be expecting that negotiation to happen, and if it doesn't, it may be an indicator that you could be looking at some options outside the company.

So, a healthy, fair, win-win long-term agreement will benefit both you and your employer.

Advice #5: Encourage and mentor others

You may know a bunch of other extraordinary persons working in your same technology, product—or even in a different one—who are not only highly knowledgable but also have started sharing their knowledge with the community.

Maybe some of them are doing it thanks to you because you invited them to speak at a certain event or to participate in some community initiative. Right?

If you still can't think of anyone, please do start today by identifying a handful of great people in your circle who have the potential and may have the passion to share valuable knowledge with the community. You might be able to identify at least one to three people.

If you already have some people in mind or when you have them, think about how transformative it could be for them to grow in the community, how much fulfilled they could feel by positively impacting others through their contributions, and potentially, in the end, follow some of your steps and become part of the MVP family. Can you imagine that? And that is, you again touching others' careers and lives.

Whenever you invite and motivate others to contribute in the community, you're bringing to them the opportunity to grow, to learn more, to expand their network, to get nurtured with the amazing energy of the community, taking their careers and their lives to unbelievable levels. Feel how fulfilling that is for you and for those who you have the chance to transform.

You already know the journey and how worthy it is. So, why not share that with others who have the potential and the right spirit as you also had when you began this journey?

I can still sadly remember when before I got to know the MVP world, I asked a current MVP at that time what it was about. I was very young, eager to learn, and connect as much as I could with others sharing the same passion. I sensed that being MVP was somehow related but honestly didn't know anything about it; so I asked him. Let's call him Charles.

He didn't answer me but dodged the question and told me that the MVP wasn't something for me. Now, several years later, when I look back and remember that episode, I can understand his reaction was a poor defense to his own ego and feeling exclusive.

Charles' reaction was very unpleasant, very far from someone who is supposed to breathe and preach community growth. But I'm grateful because when I connect the dots, I can see that episode became part of my inspiration to write this book for you as well as including this topic. I hope after reading this, you don't behave like Charles but like an actual leader, elevating those around you.

So, I exhort you to go out and share your story with as many people as you can that may be interested in hearing you, answer everyone who asks you about the MVP program, give away this book to them, support them in their journey, guide and mentor toward opportunities to volunteer and contribute.

Just one final advice on this: detach from the result of their journeys. You're not responsible for the outcomes and don't take it personally if—for any reason—they don't follow you. Your gratitude and fulfillment come by the fact of sharing your story and some opportunities with them, not by them taking action. That's not your responsibility.

However, with those who picked up your call and took action, I would suggest you cheer-lead and further mentor them so they keep up. Besides, in the case that your vendor's program accepts mentorship as a form of contribution toward your renewal, make sure you include that as well in your records.

Last but not least, do not make the mistake of nominating them for the MVP award prematurely. You already learned about that common pitfall in Chapter 2. Do not do that; it might throw overboard all the good you have made for them.

Instead, preach about passion and perseverance, about being consistent in their quantity and quality of contributions to the community, about sharing their unique and authentic value, while keeping accurate track of their records.

Advice #6: Plan for your renewal today

You did it; you reached the top, and you're starting to experience so much blessing, so many benefits for your hard work, passion, and service to the community. Can you imagine your life and your career next year without these blessings?

So, after getting awarded, and after you have realized how wonderful it is to be an MVP—given that you stay fired up about your product or technology and about giving to the community—the last thing you want is losing your MVP status.

That's partly why you learned about principles and passion at the beginning of this book; you also learned about a different way of feeling about and approaching your career. That's why I liken the process of becoming an MVP to a marathon, not a sprint toward your first award.

You really must love what you do and share your knowledge and gifts with your community, or your MVP recognition, if you ever get it, will extinguish quickly. Usually, when you start seeing signals of that waning, it may already be too late for you to renew.

Remember, your MVP recognition has a beginning and end date. It's finite. And while the period may vary depending on your vendor's program, it usually lasts just 12 months.

The point is, your MVP status does have an expiration date. When you get close to it, you'll need to submit your contributions for the last 12 months to get your MVP status renewed.

If you already have access to your vendor's website to keep your contribution records up-to-date (as is the case of Microsoft), keep an eye on the deadline for your submissions. At the moment of this writing, for instance, if you're to renew as a Microsoft MVP, you can make edits and submit your contributions until the end of March.

It's no coincidence that while *renewal* is a commonly accepted word for this process, vendors usually don't call it that. They prefer saying that you need to *reapply* for the award.

Some of them operate that way; you need to fill out a form like you did the first time—though you may be invited by default as a current MVP. Others instead, may only demand that you remain active in the community, not requiring any re-application neither submissions.

Whatever your renewal process is, trust me, you should start working on it the day after you get awarded. That way, you **avoid the last-month-before-renewal syndrome many current MVPs get stressed about.** You won't be able to contribute and do all the stuff you should have done in a year in just a month.

What's more, if you get awarded and then rest on your laurels, barely contributing to your community until you get close to your renewal period, your vendor may take that as a clear indicator that you're doing it only for the award, for the status and the privileges, not out of a true passion about the product or technology and service to the community.

So, practice what you learned in this book; especially, go over the strategic pillars in Chapter 3 and the steps and tactics outlined in Chapter 4. Be great, serve your community, enjoy the journey, keep good track of your contributions, and your MVP powers will last forever!

TAKE ACTION!
YOUR MVP POWERS

You made it! Congratulations!

Now, it's time for you to start consuming a bunch of new information that will come to you in different forms and taking advantage of new, amazing opportunities!

1. Take responsibility.

1. **Now that you are officially an MVP, keep in mind that whoever hears you speak at a conference or event, or sees your name attached to any content you publish under your signature as an MVP, will trust what you say. You're a recognized voice.**

So, first off, behave responsibly.

.... Got it!

2. **Be aware and take some time to read and complete your paperwork.**

As an MVP, you will gain access to classified information from your technology vendor. That usually means that you need to sign some NDAs (Non-Disclosure Agreements) and other contracts.

.... Done!

2. Do your initial setup and get your MVP Award kit.

1. **Depending on your vendor, upon signing some NDAs, you may be required to fill in some forms, set up your profile on your vendor's MVP website, join some exclusive mailing lists or online groups, and the like.**

.... Done!

2. **If your vendor provides a website where you can create your profile as an MVP, make sure it looks good, meaning it has your picture and as much relevant information about you as possible.**

This will help other people find you and will increase your chances of getting invited to speak at cool events and offered more opportunities.

.... Done!

3. **Confirm that your shipping information is correct so you can properly receive your well-deserved MVP Award Kit from your vendor—assuming it provides you with one.**

.... Done!

3. Get involved.

1. **It's time to figure out the new opportunities you have access to as an MVP so you can get deeply involved with your vendor, your product or technology's engineering team, and other MVP pals.**

Chances are that you will find them all exhilarating, and you'll need to prioritize.

The list of opportunities will depend on your vendor and what its MVP program offers. You will want to reach out to your Community Program Manager for the most updated information.

Here is a list of some typical opportunities. Choose no more than three or four that best resonate with you.

.... *Participate in early adoption (preview) programs.*

.... *Participate in some exclusive training or certification opportunity*

.... *Attend your exclusive MVP Summit conference.*

.... *Participate in product group interaction meetings or e-meetings with your vendor.*

.... *Speak at some of your vendor's conferences.*

.... *Subscribe to some exclusive discussion forums*

.... *Contribute some documentation or content to be posted on your vendor's website.*

.... *Submit feedback and new ideas to your vendor through a privileged channel.*

.... *Become one of the moderators of your vendor's community forum.*

.... *Others (Specify)*

....

....

....

> **2. When deciding what type of opportunities you have available and would love to get involved in, be a little choosy. Understand the prerequisites to enroll (if any) and what you need to do next.**

For example, before you get involved in early adoption programs, try to list or identify which ones are your best choices. Your decisions may be based on new features or specific modules or areas of your product that matter most to you.

Right after deciding which one or ones are most relevant for you, find out whether you meet the requirements and what steps you must take to get in.

Similarly, if you are looking forward to participating in your MVP Summit conference, then find out when and where it is going to be so you can properly budget and plan for it.

After making my choices, I commit to the following next steps.

1. ....

2. ....

3. ....

4. ....

5. ....

6. ....

7. ....

8. ....

9. ....

10. ....

4. Leverage your privileges.

Exciting, right? Well, it may sound unbelievable, but there's even more!

Yes, there are even more ways to take advantage of your MVP powers!

1. Make sure you know the shortcuts to your vendor.

For example, know your direct link with your vendor's product engineering team whenever you have a relevant issue or decision to make in your projects. Be aware also of any special form of support or special access you get with your MVP credentials.

So, after getting familiar with the communication channels and people from your vendor that participate in discussions with MVPs like you, identify and list the names of 5 key people you now can reach out to directly for help when circumstances merit.

1. Name: ....

   Role: ....

   When to contact: ....

   How: ....

2. Name: ....

   Role: ....

   When to contact: ....

   How: ....

3. Name: ....

    Role: ....

    When to contact: ....

    How: ....

4. Name: ....

    Role: ....

    When to contact: ....

    How: ....

5. Name: ....

    Role: ....

    When to contact: ....

    How: ....

Also, review your most up-to-date benefits as an MVP. You may have gained access to some type of private platform, social channel, or group that could mean a shortcut for you as an MVP to share new ideas about your product or get preferred support.

So, make sure you're aware of those shortcuts and list them here:

1. Resource/shortcut: ....

    When to use it: ....

    How to use it: ....

2. Resource/shortcut: ....

    When to use it: ....

    How to use it: ....,............

3. Resource/shortcut: ....

    When to use it: ....

    How to use it: ....,............

2. Get nurtured with invaluable world-class wisdom and connections from your MVP network.

You now get access to the best-in-class professionals worldwide who work with the same product or technology as you do. Even better, they share the same passion and community values as you do. That's why you all are MVPs, right?

So, as long as you are polite and easygoing, you would want to seek the help and opinions of other MVPs to make better decisions and find shortcuts to sort out your challenges.

After getting familiar with relevant names from your MVP network that could serve as help, I suggest you list them below so you can quickly map out who to contact when circumstances arise.

1. MVP: ....

    Speciality: ....

    How to contact: ....

2. MVP: ....

   Speciality: ....

   How to contact: ....

3. MVP: ....

   Speciality: ....

   How to contact: ....

4. MVP: ....

   Speciality: ....

   How to contact: ....

5. MVP: ....

   Speciality: ....

   How to contact: ....

6. MVP: ....

   Speciality: ....

   How to contact: ....

7. MVP: ....

   Speciality: ....

   How to contact: ....

8. MVP: ....

    Speciality: ....

    How to contact: ....

9. MVP: ....

    Speciality: ....

    How to contact: ....

10. MVP: ....

    Speciality: ....

    How to contact: ....

Feel free to increase your contact base. Switch to using a spreadsheet or more sophisticated tool as your list gets longer. You may also want to merge this list with the list of key people from your vendor.

Having a list like this not only will allow you to quickly identify who can be of great help given your circumstances, but it's also another proof of the tremendous knowledge you're bringing to the table through your MVP network when serving a customer.

Of course, do make sure you get connected with all of them through LinkedIn and other professional networks. Once again, genuinely seed your relationships with them. Try to also help them through your unique expertise whenever you have the opportunity to do so.

.... Done!

"Give the world the best you have, and the best will come back to you."

Madeline Bridges

3. Discover your additional exclusive benefits as an MVP.

Be sure to check your vendor's website and to ask your Community Program Manager and your MVP pals about more special benefits you're eligible for as an MVP.

You might have free access to software, online subscriptions, and resources provided not only by your vendor but also by other third parties.

Examples from Microsoft's MVP program are your own Office 365 subscription, credits for Azure, Visual Studio subscription, and LinkedIn learning, among several other great programs.

Several amazing third-party vendors, like TechSmith, RedGate, PluralSight, Telerik, and Infragistics, offer free licenses and specials for Microsoft MVPs.

So, first off, be sure to get familiar with special offers from your vendor and third parties. You may be surprised and want to take advantage of them all! In that case, bookmark the links relevant to you for future reference; save your notes.

.... Done!

Finally, choose up to 3 to 5 offers to take advantage of now that will significantly improve your productivity, your daily work, or your learning—and claim them!

1. ....

2. ....

3. ....

4. ....

5. ....

4. Enhance your professional profile.

Be sure to highlight your new MVP status on LinkedIn, Twitter, professional forums, other social networks you use for business, your blog or website, as well as your e-mail signature, business card, and other appropriate places.

Try to make the magic three letters (MVP) and your MVP logo as visible as possible so whoever is scanning your profile realizes you're outstanding and that you're officially recognized as a top influencer.

Use the following as a checklist of places to include your MVP tagline:

.... *LinkedIn Title and About*

.... *LinkedIn Recognitions*

.... *Your website and blog*

.... *Your vendor's or user group forums*

.... *Other social networks you use in a professional way*

.... *E-mail signature*

.... *Business card*

.... *Others (Specify)*

....

5. Wear your MVP pin and tag yourself at events.

Are you planning to attend a conference soon? Make sure to pack your MVP pin, some stickers, or whatever your vendor gifted you as part of your MVP Award Kit so you can wear them to the conference and be easily recognized as an MVP.

Whether your vendor provided you with some pin or sticker or nothing at all, try to also include the magic three letters (MVP) as part of your conference badge.

Most modern conference platforms allow you to customize the look of your conference badge during your registration, so try there first.

If none of the above suggestions apply, just handwrite "MVP" on your badge after you check-in. Yes, that should work as well.

.... Got it!

If you feel skeptical, just give it a try. Visit some sponsors that don't know you. Write your conclusions here.

....

....

....

6. Attach your recognition as part of your credentials in every commercial proposal and RFP response.

Are you working on a commercial proposal for your next project or responding to an RFP for which you and other colleagues are competing?

In addition to including your MVP award as part of your credentials, be sure to attach your MVP official recognition letter if your vendor provides one. For instance, Microsoft lets you generate a PDF online, which can be generically targeted (To Whom It May Concern) or formally targeted to a specific recipient.

If, however, your vendor doesn't provide such an option, reach out to your vendor's Community Program Manager to see whether there's a way the vendor can offer something suitable you can use, at least something generic. You lose nothing by asking!

.... Done!

If you can get or generate your generic MVP recognition letter online, I encourage you to do it now. This way, you'll have it handy to quickly attach to your upcoming commercial proposals or to forward it to customers when appropriate.

Generate your generic MVP Award Recognition Letter.

.... Done!

If you're competing for an important contract or RFP, you will want to maximize the benefits of using your recognition letter. So, generate or ask your vendor for a specific letter targeted to your customer's main contact person.

Generate your specific MVP Award Recognition Letter.

.... Done!

7. If you're self-employed, it may be a good time to reasonably increase your hourly rate.

You are more valuable now; you're a recognized professional, influential, deeply connected in your community and with your vendor, so you're saving your customers time and money.

So, review your rates, especially for new customers and consulting projects. Make sure they reflect your new status. Set your rates above average, but at the same time fair for your skills and your market.

Don't try to inadvertently increase your hourly rate for your existing customers; instead, lay out a healthy and careful plan to do so.

.... Got it!

8. If you're an employee, try to negotiate some privileges *instead of asking for an immediate increase in your salary— assuming of course that what you're receiving now is fair.*

.... *Some common privileges to negotiate with your employer are:*

.... *Funding and support for you to attend your MVP Summit conference*

.... *Funding and support for you to attend another relevant conference organized by your vendor*

.... *Permission to spend some office hours in MVP-related activities that benefit both you and your company*

.... *Empowerment to be featured as a speaker at conferences while mentioning your company*

.... *Sponsorship of some local user group meeting or community event you're organizing*

.... *Others (Specify)*

....

....

5. Encourage and mentor others.

Think of a bunch of other extraordinary persons working in the same technology, product—or even in a different one—who might enjoy contributing to the community.

Envision each of them sharing their knowledge and passion with the community and all the blessings coming their way for doing so.

Now, ask yourself what little action you can take now to help them put in that direction and start transforming their careers and, as a consequence, their lives.

Maybe it's inviting them to co-speak with you at some upcoming event or co-produce some videos with you. Maybe it's encouraging them to publish an article or some piece of code that could be helpful for the entire community. Maybe it's connecting them with someone else.

What is it that you can do NOW for them and help them grow in the community? Think about that and write your thoughts below:

1) Person's name: ....

I think he/she must share with the community about . . .

....

And this is how I will help him/her to do so NOW . . .

....

2) Person's name: ....

I think he/she must share with the community about . . .

....

And this is how I will help him/her to do so NOW . . .

....

3) Person's name: ....

I think he/she must share with the community about . . .

....

And this is how I will help him/her to do so NOW . . .

....

6. Plan for your renewal today.

Remember, your MVP recognition has a beginning and end date. It's finite. While the period may vary depending on your vendor's program, it usually lasts about 12 months.

> **1. After getting awarded and have realized how wonderful it is to be an MVP, given you stay fired up about your product or technology and about giving to the community, you won't want to lose your MVP status.**

So, don't rest on your laurels. Contribute regularly and do keep good records of all your contributions. You'll need those records sooner than later.

Be mindful of how your vendor's MVP renewal process works as well as the time frame.

.... Got it!

> **2. I recommend you set up monthly T-minus alerts that remind and help you to be mindful and regularly measure your performance toward your renewal as an MVP.**

.... Done!

> **3. Whether or not your vendor has a questionnaire for you to complete (Microsoft does), ask yourself the following questions before applying for your renewal:**

Why do you want to continue to be an MVP?

....

....

What are the most impactful community contributions you've made in the last year?

....

....

What significant impact do you plan to make on the community in the upcoming year?

....

....

What are you doing to make your community better (e.g., charity work, diversity and inclusion efforts, education, mentoring)?

....

....

....

7 SUMMARY

"You can't connect the dots looking forward; you can only connect them looking backwards. So you have to trust that the dots will somehow connect in your future."

Steve Jobs

Most Valuable Professionals, or MVPs, are technology experts who passionately share their knowledge with the community and are officially recognized by their technology vendor.

SAP calls them *Champions*, Oracle refers to them as *ACEs*, Google as *Developer Experts*, Amazon (AWS) as *Heroes*.

The program's name could vary from vendor to vendor and over time, but the essence doesn't. **Most Valuable Professionals, or MVPs, Champions, ACEs, Experts, Heroes are all extraordinary professionals driven by passion about their vendor's products and sharing knowledge with their communities.**

The keyword here is **passion.** You will need it throughout your MVP journey, which you should consider more like a marathon than a sprint.

The MVP award is not about a final destination you intend to reach, but it's about an exciting way of living your career and your life. You'll be spending a lot more time on the journey than you will at the ultimate destination, which, in reality, is not ultimate at all—it usually lasts just for 12 months—and you should keep it up positively impacting your community to get renewed again.

There's no straightforward process for getting awarded either, at least not from any technology vendor at this moment. However, we can identify 5 common key elements about what it takes to become an MVP according to different vendors:

- Committing to learning more every day about your vendor's products.

- Loving what you do and helping others.

- Contributing and sharing knowledge with the community.

- Leading and being a positive influencer.

- And finally, as an inevitable consequence of persistently doing all of the above, getting nominated by someone else.

You depend on getting nominated—or recruited—by someone else, so designated people within your vendor—and other MVPs in some cases—can evaluate the impact of your community contributions and vote.

Principles

If you identify with the basic principles that follow and want to commit to them, then you may be MVP material.

- Genuine community spirit. The only reason for being an MVP is to serve your community just for the sake of it.

- Passion. If you are not passionate about your technology or product of choice, becoming an MVP will be such a burden for you that you probably will give up trying.

- Desire to transcend. You must believe that you're called to do better, to truly make a difference in your community.

- Willpower. Your MVP journey won't be free. There's a price you will need to pay—maybe not directly in the form of money but in some tradeoffs you will need to make to achieve your MVP goals.

By living the above core principles and by consistently applying some valuable strategies and concrete steps you learned in this book, you might have a better chance of succeeding, whether your goal is to become an MVP for the first time, to get renewed or simply level up in your career.

Foundational questions

Before continuing, ask yourself the following foundational questions to determine whether aspiring to become an MVP truly resonates with you:

- Are you passionate about your product or technology?

- Are you passionate about sharing knowledge with like-minded people and selflessly helping others, or do you want to become an MVP just for the prize, status, and benefits?

- What is your real purpose for aspiring to become an MVP? What is your "why"?

- Are you willing to pay the price?

- Will becoming an MVP make you happy?

Myths

There are also some **myths and misbeliefs** about MVPs that were debunked in this book. For example:

- Being an MVP doesn't mean you have to be the guru in your area of expertise. Just start contributing from where you are now.

- Public speaking is just one of the possible ways to contribute to your community. So, don't worry about it if speaking in front of an audience freaks you out or just doesn't resonate with you.

- MVPs do make mistakes as you and I do every day, so don't pursue perfection; instead, seek an attitude of imperfectly sharing value with your peers.

- MVP isn't a certification on your technology or product. There's no official exam attached neither judgment of your knowledge but for your contributions to the community.

- Money is not part of the equation for MVP contributions, at least in the sense of making a profit from them. (In some cases, asking for money is fine to cover some costs or charging a small entry fee to ensure attendance, but the end goal is not to generate profit.)

Many MVP aspirants fail in their attempt to become MVPs. Some try for years until they just give up. I hope you don't fall into any of those categories, and you succeed in your goal.

Common pitfalls

Some of the most common pitfalls MVP aspirants make and you should avoid are:

- Having the wrong attitude. If being an MVP for you means status and recognition instead of passion and community service, you are taking the wrong path.

- Overcrowded category. While you must choose according to your passion, you should remember that the more established your MVP award category is and the more MVPs that already participate in it, the harder it will be for you to get awarded.

- Overlooking the geography factor. How many MVPs in your field are located in your country and region? Similar to the preceding item, the more there are and the higher their caliber, the harder it will be for you to stand out.

- Premature nomination. You must be patient. In the case of nominations, remember that getting nominated before having a track record of at least 12 consecutive months of constant community contributions is a fast lane toward getting rejected.

- Lack of self-discipline. Self-discipline is crucial. If you don't change some bad habits and discipline yourself to consistently serve your community, commit to constant learning, and persevere in passionately sharing your knowledge, odds are that you will never step on the MVP podium.

- Poor or no strategy. You may have the right attitude, passion, knowledge, desire for personal and professional growth, and even self-discipline, but if you don't execute well, if you don't implement a good strategy, you could end up not being nominated—or recruited by your vendor—or failing nomination after nomination.

Four strategic pillars

In Chapter 3, you learned about the **four strategic pillars** I followed for years, which have proven to work for others as well.

Strategic Pillar #1: Focus.

You cannot be a generalist if you desire to lift the MVP trophy.

Smartly choose your MVP technology award category, and specifically the product, sub-product, platform, or module you enjoy; pursue a strong desire to excel, and stand out through your contributions.

It doesn't mean that you shouldn't touch or refer to complementary technologies, but you need to choose one for your primary focus— the one that will be part of your identity and will predominate in your MVP contributions.

Strategic Pillar #2: Impact.

Remember the three key variables that will be considered in the evaluation of your contributions:

Authenticity

Share your truly unique talents with your community. **There's no point pretending to be somebody else.** Be yourself; be authentic.

What works for others may not necessarily work for you. So, find your own style when contributing. Author your own content in whatever form it takes (e.g., article, talk, video, course, code).

Your content is part of your identity and determines how much value you provide. So, **tell your own stories and focus on quality over quantity**. Do not copy and paste the content of others.

Value

Do not pursue perfection; that's an illusion.

While you should check you're not making obvious technical or conceptual mistakes, get hooked on providing real value to your audience. Value is what it's all about.

Your community is eager to receive your real-world advice, tips, best practices, good solutions, and workarounds to real challenges.

Give your community members what they expect from an MVP!

Reach

There is no sense in creating amazing content if nobody (or just very few people among your community) is aware of it.

So, unless you want to enter the business of creating audiences for some other purposes (which usually takes years of perseverance and money), I would strongly recommend that you take advantage of existing channels where your audience is already hanging out and is readily available to you (e.g., existing user groups, events in your area, conferences, magazines, online communities or open-source projects).

Strategic Pillar #3: Commitment.

> *"Motivation is what gets you started; habit is what keeps you going."*

Jim Rohn

As you learned in Chapter 2, lack of self-discipline is one of the common mistakes most aspiring and renewing MVPs make.

To achieve your MVP award goals, cultivating the habit of regularly contributing to your community is indispensable, and the more quality and value you provide, the better. Never put quantity over quality. It doesn't make any sense.

You may reserve some time every day or week, maybe a few hours during weekends, or part of your lunchtime—whatever works best for you. Plan for it. Commit to it. Start and adjust on the go if needed.

Strategic Pillar #4: Records.

The lack of good records of community contributions is sadly one of the most common reasons why some of those who deserve being awarded (or renewed) as MVPs just don't make it.

Being a great contributor in your community, while necessary, is not enough for those aspiring to become an MVP or get renewed. You also need to prove it.

That is why keeping records of ALL your contributions and their positive impact is as critical as the act of contributing. Keep in mind that accurate records encompass quantity as well as quality.

Some techniques that have proven to work for me are:

- Log your contributions right away or even before they happen.

- Log them directly in your vendor's MVP system designed for that purpose if you already have access to it.

- Use your custom Spreadsheet that includes at least the title, technology, status, date, type, URL, and a measure of the impact of each of your contributions.

Note: Feel welcome to try the MVP Log & Planner spreadsheet I've created for you to start tracking your contributions. You can download it free of charge from here: **https://www.becomemvp.com**

- Leverage productivity tools like Evernote, OneNote, and similars that let you quickly bookmark websites, articles, taking notes, capture screenshots, etc.

Logging in whatever form works best for you, make sure you don't neglect to include any of your great contributions. These will serve both as your credentials and reminders of your exciting journey toward your first MVP nomination or renewal.

Your journey

Your MVP journey is not a straightforward one and depends on a lot of variables. What worked for me and others may not be what works for you. Your path might be different.

However, there are 8 steps that might significantly increase your chances of getting a nomination. These were covered in detail in Chapter 4.

The steps are (in any order except the first one) as follows:

Step #1: Be Present Where People Need You.

Find and join the spaces today where those you want to serve are hanging out. Especially, seek out those who are starting and are eager to be educated, guided, helped, and served by someone of your caliber.

Some common places are user group meetings, conferences, local events hosted by your vendor, online forums, meet-ups, and groups in social networks.

The more people you get exposed to, the more opportunities you will have to share your passion, contribute, generate impact, gain new followers and supporters, and even surround yourself with positive energy.

Step #2: Volunteer.

Volunteering is about raising your hand to offer some help to improve your community, usually in your same area or region. It's leadership in action!

From offering yourself to speak at an upcoming event to serving on a programming committee, showcase your leadership skills while you improve your community, your career, and your chances of becoming visible to people who will support your journey.

Step #3: Contribute Content.

Content is king and comprises real proof of your knowledge and passion around your product or technology of choice.

Contributing content doesn't require you to be a keynote speaker neither a technical guru. **It just requires courage, determination, and discipline.**

Pursue sharing concrete value, your real findings, and solutions to common challenges.

Your contribution may be delivering a session at an upcoming event, or it might be giving a series of webinars, writing articles, answering questions in forums, and the like.

Find the format and platform that resonates with you. You can always try a different format later, but you may not know what works best for you until you try it.

Get rid of any roadblocks. Take advantage of channels where you don't need to worry about infrastructure issues or how to bring in audiences. Go for established user groups, forums, and events where audiences are already there, eager for your content.

Step #4: Find Your Mentors.

On your MVP journey, you should seek out and choose a handful of current MVPs to learn from and to model their best practices.

Don't be afraid to reach out to some of those you follow on the

Internet. Introduce yourself, tell them that you're committed to becoming an MVP and that you would appreciate some mentorship.

Try to get more than one (ideally, three different mentors) so you can take advantage of the diversity of opinions, types of connections, and opportunities they can bring you.

Step #5: Share Feedback and Ideas With Your Vendor.

Is there some extraordinary feature that could improve the vendor's technology in a way that wasn't initially thought of, which could open doors to a whole new world of possibilities?

Is there any preview or beta program from your vendor about some upcoming cool new version or functionality of your product that you could join and contribute with your ideas?

Giving honest feedback through your technology vendor's approved channels not only gives you and your peers the chance to receive in return what you ask for but also turns you into someone who raises his or her voice for the benefit of others. That's part of the process of becoming a thought leader—a key attribute of an MVP.

Besides, make sure to reach out to Product Managers and Architects from your vendor who might be present at conferences to discuss directly with them your product ideas.

Step #6: Be YOU The Change.

Wherever you find a gap, that might be your next fascinating step on your MVP journey: your opportunity to create a change, to lead a movement.

The opportunity may be starting a local user group, hosting a new online event, taking on a code project, starting an online community in your local language, or something else.

Creating and leading a movement requires a combination of volunteering, contributing, leadership, and entrepreneurial spirit to achieve something amazing for your community.

If you are willing to commit what it takes, starting a new movement could be fascinating. The venture will become part of your DNA as a thought leader in your community and your legacy for others.

Step #7: Connect With Your Community Program Manager.

A representative of your vendor is dedicated to recruiting and developing new MVPs in your region or worldwide. It's part of your mission to find and start hanging out with that person.

By approaching the Community Program Manager, you're contributing to that person's goals, so you're saving him or her time and effort. You're the shortcut to that person's success, so he or she will respond to you.

That person is also a shortcut for you because he or she is in the best position to provide you with key information and opportunities for becoming a first-time MVP or getting renewed.

Step #8: Keep Up Contributing And Be Patient.

As a general rule, MVP programs consider your last 12 months' performance. Thus, if your vendor grants MVP awards through a nomination process, I recommend you don't knock on its door unless you have real proof that you consistently created a positive impact in the community during at least the last 12 months.

So, keep up contributing and be patient! If you're truly passionate about your product or technology from your vendor, you're committed to growing personally and professionally every day, you love sharing knowledge with others, you have a genuine desire to serve your community, and you're doing what it takes, odds are, you will be nominated (or included in some private list of candidates for the award) sooner or later.

Your nomination

"Getting nominated is the inevitable consequence of consistently sharing your passion and your knowledge with the community, not the driver."

Pablo Peralta

Receiving and reviewing nominations is the most usual mechanism through which tech vendors award their top community contributors. However, the nomination process may vary from vendor to vendor and over time.

In Chapter 5, you learned about the 5 common phases nomination processes consist of according to most vendors and what you need to know before getting nominated.

Phase #1: Meet The Requirements.

Actively contribute to the community for a minimum of 12 months and make sure you meet all the requirements determined by your vendor.

Do not rush to meet their next nominations period of your vendor. Do not make the mistake of getting a premature nomination, as I described in *Chapter 2*. If you don't feel 100% ready, odds are it's because you aren't yet.

Phase #2: Get Nominated And Fill In Your Application.

Get nominated (usually by another MVP, customer, or vendor's

FTE) and fill in the information requested by your vendor. It usually requires you to create your account within your vendor's MVP web platform or complete an online form.

Whatever the case, you will need to list your contributions and share proof of how you have positively impacted your community during the last 12 months.

That's why, anew, keeping up to date your log is so crucial. You don't want to trust your memory for this unbelievable moment in your career.

Phase #3: Your Vendor's Review.

Getting nominated (or in your vendors' candidate list for the award) doesn't guarantee you'll be awarded by them. What it means is that now you're much more visible to them, and your contributions and behaviors as a thought leader will be evaluated.

Different members of your vendor's team (and sometimes others MVPs as well) will be reviewing your nomination and finally deciding if you deserve the award at this time or not. This process usually takes up to 90 days.

Meanwhile, the best thing you can do is to keep demonstrating your commitment to improving your community and why you should be awarded among those that are on the same list as you.

The process isn't much different if you're seeking renewal as an existent MVP, except that you don't need to get nominated again, but you 'just' go through your annual review phase.

Phase #4: Your Vendor's Notifications And Announcements.

Your vendor will notify you about the result of your nomination and will publicly announce awarded MVPs.

It usually takes up to 90 days after you supply all the information or their period to accept nominations ends.

Besides, your vendor may use specific months or days for announcing the award winners. In any case, you should be the first one to get notified if you got awarded (or not) some hours before it makes their public announcements.

Phase #5: Celebrate or Re-apply Later.

You couldn't make it this time?

Don't worry! Most new aspirants don't make it their first time out. You can usually apply later according to your vendor's timeframes and requirements.

Make sure to understand what you missed, what you need to improve or adjust for your next application and persevere on your MVP journey!

Did you make it? Celebrate your MVP status and be grateful!

Congratulations! You've got new powers! You're an MVP—one of the top influencers of your product or technology worldwide!

So, first, celebrate and give thanks to those who accompanied you on your MVP journey.

Second, honor the phrase "with great power comes great responsibility." Put your powers at the service of your community, not at the service of your ego.

Making the most of your MVP powers

Here is a summary of the advice you learned in Chapter 6 about making the most of your MVP powers.

Advice #1: Take Responsibility.

You're an official thought leader in your area of expertise now. Whoever hears you speak at some conference or event or sees your name attached to any publication, content, or even social post will know that it's coming from a recognized source.

In essence, any opinion you make in any public space gains much more attention now. So, pursue integrity as a thought leader and honor your MVP status, NDAs, and other contracts. Be responsible.

Advice #2: Do Your Initial Setup and Get Your MVP Award Kit.

If this is your first time as an MVP, chances are that you are starting to receive tons of e-mail, invitations, opportunities, forms to fill in, contracts to sign, and the like.

Your first task is to do your initial setup. Make sure you're ready. Depending on your vendor, after signing an NDA contract, you may be required to fill in some forms, set up your profile on your vendor's MVP website, join some exclusive mailing list or online group, and so forth.

Only after completing your initial setup will your vendor have the information required to ship any MVP Award Kit the company has prepared for you.

Advice #3: Get Involved.

After finishing up your setup as an MVP, you will want to get familiar with the new opportunities you have in front of you to get involved and take your talents and passion to new levels.

There are plenty of fascinating choices, such as participating in exclusive early adoption programs, MVPs-only workshops, and certification programs, interacting frequently and directly with your vendor's product team, submitting new ideas, considering opportunities to speak at relevant conferences organized by your vendor, leading content creation initiatives, and attending your exclusive MVP Summit.

Getting involved in most of these will also grow your list of contributions for your next period renewal. But be selective; odds are that you won't have enough time to enroll in everything you would like.

Particularly, I encourage you to participate in opportunities where you can learn more and hang out with your MVP pals (e.g., at your exclusive MVP Summit conference) and with your vendor's product team.

It's best to start with opportunities that don't demand a lot of time commitment from you upfront.

Advice #4: Leverage Your Privileges.

Exciting, right? Well, it may seem unbelievable, but there's even more!

Yes, there are even more ways to take advantage of your MVP powers! Some examples are:

- Shortcuts. Enjoy the direct relationship with your vendor's product team whenever you have a relevant issue or decision to make in your projects. Be sure your customers are aware that you know the names and numbers of who to speak with when the need arises. That's valuable time and money you're saving them on projects. It's part of your competitive advantage as an MVP.

- Get nurtured with invaluable world-class wisdom and connections from your MVP network. You now belong to a network that is comprised of the best-in-class professionals in your area of expertise around the globe, who share your same passion and values. Try to contribute whenever possible, and be sure to use this resource whenever needed. Also, ensure that your customers know you have that power!

- Discover your additional exclusive benefits as an MVP —if any—. For example, these may include free licenses and online subscriptions for amazing third-party software products, great learning tools, and resources, and vouchers to take official exams.

- Enhance your professional profile. Be sure to highlight your MVP title in your online profiles such as LinkedIn, on your business card, in your professional curriculum, and other appropriate places.

- Wear your MVP pin, if you received one from your vendor, and tag yourself at events. Use stickers and even handwrite on your next conference badge to add your MVP tagline. Try it out at your next conference and see how powerful this technique is!

- Attach your recognition letter (if your vendor provides one like Microsoft does) to your next commercial proposal or RFP response.

- If you're self-employed, it may be a good time to reasonably increase your hourly rate. Your work is of higher value now; you're a recognized professional, influential, deeply connected in your community and with your vendor, so you're delivering more to your customers.

- If you're an employee, try to negotiate some privileges such as dedicating office hours to MVP activities and gaining the needed support to attend your MVP Summit conference and some other relevant conferences organized by your vendor.

Advice #5: Encourage and Mentor Others.

Think of a bunch of other extraordinary persons working in the same technology, product—or even in a different one—who might enjoy contributing to the community.

Whenever you invite and motivate others to contribute in the community, you're bringing to them the opportunity to grow, to learn more, to expand their network, to get nurtured with the amazing energy of the community, taking their careers and their lives to unbelievable levels. Feel how fulfilling that is for you and for those who you have the chance to transform.

I encourage you to share your story, give away this book to them, guide, and mentor toward opportunities to volunteer and contribute.

Advice #6: Plan for Your Renewal Today.

After getting awarded and after you have realized how wonderful it is to be an MVP, stay fired up about your product or technology, and about community giving. You want to hold onto your MVP status.

Remember, your MVP recognition has a beginning and end date. It's a finite period, and while it may vary depending on your vendor's program, it usually lasts just 12 months.

So, don't rest on your laurels. Light up your passion and community spirit. Contribute frequently and endeavor to keep good records of all your contributions. You'll need those records later.

Be aware of how your vendor's MVP renewal process works as well as the time frame.

Take a moment to reflect and ask yourself:

- Why do you want to continue to be an MVP?

- What are the most impactful community contributions you've made in the last year?

- What significant impact do you plan to make on the community in the upcoming year?

- What are you doing to make your community better (e.g., charity work, diversity and inclusion efforts, education, mentoring)?

CLOSING THOUGHTS

Becoming a Most Valuable Professional (MVP)—or whatever name your vendor uses to refer to these recognized individuals—in your area of expertise is about taking your career and life to a whole new level.

It's about committing yourself to growth, actively leading, and passionately sharing knowledge with your community.

As an MVP, you belong to a group of very few carefully chosen experts around the globe who decided to make a difference, to be the content creators rather than the consumers. That decision and determination led to recognition by their technology vendor and access to unbelievable benefits and privileges.

Nevertheless, becoming an MVP isn't the destination and shouldn't be for the award itself. That won't get you there; neither will it keep you there. The award is a consequence of your passion, unselfish help, and contributions to your community. Don't forget that.

You don't need to be the guru in your product or technology; neither must you be a conference keynote speaker. You can start where you are now—just by sharing valuable, authentic lessons you've learned, through the channels you feel most comfortable with.

I hope this book has provided you with some inspiration and useful advice to start your MVP journey or to put yourself back on track.

Just remember one more thing: You must enjoy the journey. You will spend much more time on it than at your final destination.

So, choose a technology or product that moves you; embrace opportunities to share your passion with like-minded people, and put your talents at the service of your community. It's so powerful, so fulfilling. Chances are that soon, you'll see how it transforms your career and your life—with or without the award.

You don't know how far your MVP journey will take you, but now that you have read this book and are about to take action, I look forward to your future success. You now know where and when to start—and that's right here, right now. Engage!

APPENDIX A

Resources

Download your MVP Log & Planner Spreadsheet FREE of charge here:

https://www.becomemvp.com

From that same site, you will also find additional training and resources to support your MVP journey as I make them available.

Make sure to subscribe so you're first to know when I release something new.

APPENDIX B

MVP Programs

Amazon AWS Heroes Program

https://aws.amazon.com/developer/community/heroes/

Embarcadero MVP Program

https://www.embarcadero.com/es/embarcadero-mvp-program

Find an Embarcadero MVP:
https://www.embarcadero.com/es/partners/mvp-directory

Nominate an Embarcadero MVP:
https://www.embarcadero.com/es/nominating-an-mvp

Google Experts Program

https://developers.google.com/community/experts

Find a Google expert:
https://developers.google.com/community/experts/directory

Microsoft MVP Program

https://mvp.microsoft.com

Find a Microsoft MVP:
https://mvp.microsoft.com/en-us/MvpSearch

Find the MVP Award Structure:
https://mvp.microsoft.com/en-us/Pages/mvp-award-update

Nominate a Microsoft MVP:
https://mvp.microsoft.com/en-us/Nomination/nominate-an-mvp

Oracle ACE Program

https://www.oracle.com/technetwork/community/oracle-ace

Find an Oracle ACE:
https://apex.oracle.com/pls/apex/f?p=19297:3:

Nominate an Oracle ACE:
https://www.oracle.com/technetwork/community/oracle-ace/
become-an-ace

Salesforce MVP Program

https://www.salesforce.com/campaign/mvp

Find a Salesforce MVP:
https://success.salesforce.com/mvp

SAP Champions Program

https://community.sap.com/programs/influencer-programs/
champions

Find an SAP champion:
https://community.sap.com/influencers/?program=sapchampions

Sitecore MVP Program

https://mvp.sitecore.com

Sitecore 2020 MVPs
http://mvp.sitecore.com/MVPs/2020

Sitecore MVP Nomination process:
https://mvp.sitecore.com/become-an-mvp

Can't find your technology vendor's MVP program? Any omissions or errors? If you would like to contribute to this list, please e-mail me at

pabloperalta@live.com

GLOSSARY

Community Program Manager

A technology vendor's internal employee who manages the company's community-awards program and nominations within an area or region.

Depending on your vendor, this person's title may vary.

MVP Program

The program developed by a technology vendor to choose and recognize its best community members based on their contributions. Commonly, it's referred to as the MVP Program by Microsoft and other vendors, but you can also find some variants. For instance, Oracle calls its program the ACE Program; for SAP, it's the Champions Program; Google refers to it as the Experts Program, Amazon as Heroes.

For this book, most of the time, it's just referred to as the MVP program.

MVP Award Category

Award categories encompass technology products and areas of specialization for which you can be awarded according to your contributions.

Depending on your vendor's MVP program, the categories can be as simple and linear as by individual products, or each category can encompass several products and technologies.

For instance, in the case of Microsoft, there is an award category for

Data Platform, where contributing to technologies like SQL Server, Azure SQL, Power BI, and so forth, add up for your recognition.

For more information on Microsoft MVP award categories, visit **https://mvp.microsoft.com/en-us/Pages/mvp-award-update**

Other vendors, like SAP, have categories (called focus groups) such as SAP Cloud Platform, Big Data, and DDM & Analytics/SAP HANA.

Sitecore, instead, has three categories at the moment of this writing: Technology—for its traditional technology; Commerce—specific to its Sitecore Ecommerce technology; and Strategy—for those contributors more on the business than on the technology side.

Product or Technology of Your Choice

The software product, platform, programming language, or technology you choose to become expert in and aspire to get recognized for. For instance, Windows, SQL Server, Power BI, Office 365, .Net, SAP HANA, Oracle Database, Java.

Depending on your vendor's community-awards program, your choice could represent an award category in itself or may be part of a broader category.

Vendor (or Technology Vendor)

A technology company that sells products (usually software products) and has community programs to recognize its best evangelizers and contributors around the world. For example, Microsoft, Salesforce, Sitecore, Embarcadero, Oracle, SAP, Amazon, and Google.

ACKNOWLEDGMENTS

This book would not have been possible without the support and encouragement of my wife, Silvana.

For understanding my extended hours and weekends at the computer, I would like to thank my children: Juan Angel, Josefina, and Mathias.

Words cannot express my gratitude to Microsoft and its MVP program for supporting my growth as a professional, and mostly as an individual, enjoying and learning from great friends all around the world.

Special thanks to my mentor, Tony Stein, who believed in me and gave me the opportunity to dedicate part of my life to serve communities.

To those who dedicated their time to share sincere feedback about this craft and how to improve it: Craig Cmehil, Tamas Varga, Becky de Loryn, Glauter Januzzi, Cristina González Herrero, Enrique Romero, Daniel Montiel, Emmanuel David Rodríguez Hernández, Borja Prado, Javier Menendez Pallo.

I would particularly like to thank Tamas Varga and Sitecore for providing not only deep feedback about this book but also contributing additional information, pics, and resources from its program that I am including in this book.

None of this would have been possible without the exceptional help from my editors Tessy and Kathie-Jo Arnoff and my designer, Petya Tsankova.

ABOUT THE AUTHOR

PABLO PERALTA is a tech entrepreneur and knowledge broker who loves participating in and creating communities. Due to his unique consistent contributions as an event speaker and organizer, instructor, writer, forum moderator, and other volunteer leadership positions, he was recognized by Microsoft as a Most Valuable Professional (MVP) in 2010, which was his first time to receive this honor, and has renewed this recognition every year since.

In 2012, Pablo founded Comunidad365, the #1 Spanish-speaking community related to Microsoft Business Solutions—later acquired by Dynamic Communities, Inc.—serving as a platform for hundreds of great individuals to openly connect, learn, and share their passion for Microsoft products.

It was especially through that platform that Pablo made several amazing new friends and had the blessing to mentor some of them to finally get awarded as MVPs because of their great contributions to the community.

Pablo embraced the mission of inspiring extraordinary leaders like you to succeed in their desire to share their knowledge with the community and become better selves.

That's why he endeavored in creating and organizing so many successful educational programs and tech events that reach the masses, both online and in-person.

If you are committed to achieving great things in your tech community and would like some professional advice, do not hesitate in reaching out to him.

Connect with Pablo:

LinkedIn:	**www.linkedin.com/in/pabloperalta**
Twitter:	**twitter.com/pabloperalta**
Email:	**pabloperalta@live.com**

ONE LAST THING!

To make sure this book performs well on Amazon, it's vital that I get as many authentic and useful reviews as possible.

That's why if you enjoyed this book or found it useful, I would be very grateful if you would post a review on Amazon. Please include in your review what you found more useful in the book.

You can also mark reviews from others as helpful.

Your support really does make a difference. I read all the reviews personally so I can get your feedback and make this book even better.

Thanks again for your support!